UNCOVE
EAP

Teaching academic writing and reading

Sam McCarter & Phil Jakes

Macmillan Education
Between Towns Road, Oxford OX4 3PP
A division of Macmillan Publishers Limited
Companies and representatives throughout the world

ISBN 978-0-2307-2322-1

Note to Teachers

Permission to copy

The material in this book is copyright. However,
the publisher grants permission for copies to be
made without fee on those pages marked with the
photocopiable symbol.

Private purchasers may make copies for their own
use or for use by classes of which they are in charge;
school purchasers may make copies for use within
and by the staff and students of the school only. This
permission does not extend to additional branches of
an institution, who should purchase a separate master
copy of the book for their own use.

For copying in any other circumstances, prior
permission in writing must be obtained from
Macmillan Publishers Limited.

Designed by Anne Davies
Illustrated by Julian Mosedale
Cover design by Macmillan Publishers Limited
Cover photograph by Getty Images/Philippe Bourseiller

The publishers would like to thank Professor John
Flowerdew and Liz Hunt for their thoughtful insights
and recommendations.

The authors and publishers would like to thank
the following for permission to reproduce their
photographs:
Alamy/Corbis Premium RF p102(tr), Alamy/Les
Gibbon p102(tl), Alamy/SCPhotos p102 (bl);
Corbis/Gideon Mendel for Action Aid p79;
Getty Images/Doable/A.collection p102 (br);
Wiley-Blackwell/Kaplan's diagram of cross-cultural
differences in paragraph organization/ R.B Kaplan/
Copyright © 1966. Reproduced with kind permission of
Blackwell Publishing Ltd p13;

The authors and publishers are grateful for permission
to reprint the following copyright material:

Reproduced with the permission of Nelson Thornes
from *The New Wider World* by David Waugh, first
printed in 1998;

The Economist for an extract from 'The financial crisis:
What Next?' published in *The Economist* 18 September
2008 copyright © The Economist Newspaper Limited,
London 2008.

These materials may contain links for third party
websites. We have no control over, and are not
responsible for, the contents of such third party websites.
Please use care when accessing them.

Although we have tried to trace and contact copyright
holders before publication, in some cases this has not
been possible. If contacted we will be pleased to rectify
any errors or omissions at the earliest opportunity.

Printed and bound in China

2013 2012 2011 2010 2009
10 9 8 7 6 5 4 3 2 1

Contents

About the authors

Sam McCarter

Sam McCarter's teaching career spans a period of more than 30 years. His first teaching post was as a volunteer English teacher with Voluntary Services Overseas (VSO) in Sierra Leone, West Africa. He has taught a wide range of subjects ranging from classical to medieval ecclesiastical Latin and from basic literacy to academic English and ESP.

Sam has been writing, teaching and editing academic English and English for Medical Purposes for more than 15 years. The author of several textbooks, Sam has also edited glossaries for CD-ROMs on tropical medicine. He now devotes his time to writing and teaching academic English and ESP via videoconferencing.

Phil Jakes

Phil Jakes has extensive experience of ESOL, EAP and teacher training and has worked in the Middle East and the UK, in both the private and state sectors. He has worked on a range of EAP courses including foundation courses, in-course language support for degree-level and postgraduate students, pre-sessional subject-specific courses and IELTS preparation classes. This has given him a keen understanding of the needs of students from a wide range of backgrounds. He feels that success in the planning and delivery of EAP teaching and training depends on a student-centred approach at all stages.

About the series

Macmillan Books for Teachers

Welcome to Macmillan Books for Teachers. The titles are written by acknowledged and innovative leaders in each field to help you develop your teaching repertoire, practical skill and theoretical knowledge.

Suited to both newer and to more experienced teachers, the series combines the best of classic teaching methodology with recent, cutting-edge developments. Insights from academic research are combined with hands-on experience to create books which focus on real-world teaching solutions.

We hope you will find the ideas in them a source of inspiration in your own teaching and enjoyment in your professional learning.

Adrian Underhill

Titles in the series

500 Activities for the Primary Classroom
Carol Read

700 Classroom Activities
David Seymour & Maria Popova

An A–Z of ELT
Scott Thornbury

Blended Learning
Barney Barrett & Pete Sharma

Beyond the Sentence
Scott Thornbury

Children Learning English
Jayne Moon

Discover English
Rod Bolitho & Brian Tomlinson

Learning Teaching
Jim Scrivener

Sound Foundations
Adrian Underhill

Teaching Practice
Roger Gower, Diane Phillips & Steve Walters

Teaching Reading Skills
Christine Nuttall

Uncovering CLIL
Peeter Mehisto, David Marsh & María Jesús Frigols

Uncovering Grammar
Scott Thornbury

Foreword

Using English in higher education is now a fact of life for students around the world, whether studying their subjects in English as a second language in their home country, or studying as international students in English-medium colleges and universities. For these students, adequate facility with English for Academic Purposes (EAP) has become a prerequisite to success.

This places an increased demand on English-language teachers who want to prepare their students to take full advantage of their subject-related studies in English, to enable them to access resources in English, to enter their subject discourse in English with confidence, and to present written work in English to the required standards (and consequently to find their studies more satisfying and less stressful).

However, English-language teachers are themselves often thrown in at the deep end, having little training in what an EAP syllabus should consist of or how to teach it. Moreover, English-language teachers are often faced with limited resources with which to offer the quality of instruction they wish for, and limited time in which to meet the various competing language and exam needs of their students. This handbook is designed and written precisely for those teachers.

Sam McCarter and Phil Jakes bring together an enormous and varied experience of working with students of EAP across many cultures, and of helping teachers to develop confidence and skill in all relevant techniques for enabling students to master EAP to the required level. They distil that experience into this practical handbook in which they offer, within each chapter:

- insights into the components of EAP, to act as a map of the territory of EAP;
- examples of good practice, to see that doing it well is entirely possible;
- a range of activities for developing confidence in each subset of EAP skills – immediate, useable, relevant classroom resources.

The authors cover the full spectrum of EAP from academic reading to research, from understanding assignments to selecting and synthesising ideas and presenting critical arguments, from redrafting to referencing, and the relation of EAP to ESP. In addition they frame all this within current developments in EAP and the special needs of the new generation of international students.

Embedded in the text is the constant understanding of the linguistic and thinking challenges presented by the double demand of English and of academia. Even native-English-speaking students can be challenged by the academic demands of higher education, so it is very important that we teachers equip ourselves to prepare students who are non-native speakers of English to make the most of their educational opportunities, and to have equal access to success in the global village. This handbook will enable teachers to help their students to do this.

Adrian Underhill

Series Editor

Introduction

Whether you are new to English for Academic Purposes (EAP), an experienced EAP teacher, a native speaker or a non-native speaker of English, and no matter where you are in the world, this book will be a useful companion, providing you with practical ideas and tips that cross cultures and borders.

EAP is the English that is taught to second-/third-language students at various educational establishments including high schools and private language schools as they prepare to enter universities and other institutions of higher education. As the teaching of EAP spreads to different institutions, more and more teachers are being asked to prepare students for university – or indeed help students already enrolled in university courses – without the benefit of any prior knowledge or training. This book aims to provide a gentle introduction to those of you who find yourselves in this situation.

If you have been teaching EAP for a while and need some extra guidance and support, or even confirmation that you are following the right path, you will find plenty of ideas and activities that are of use. While this book is aimed primarily at teachers of EAP, many IELTS teachers may also find the information and techniques outlined of some use as they prepare their students for the IELTS exam and for entry to university courses.

Each chapter contains a theory section, a *Good practice* example and a bank of activities. All suggestions and tips are pooled from the authors' combined experience, which totals more than 50 years of teaching adults at different levels and from various backgrounds in disciplines ranging from basic skills to EAP, English for Special Purposes (ESP) and English for Occupational Purposes (EOP), at undergraduate and postgraduate levels.

In the first part of each chapter you will find basic theoretical input on key topics such as critical thinking, types of writing and giving feedback. In this theoretical section we offer an easy-to-follow, jargon-free introduction to EAP teaching, interspersed with practical tips.

The *Good practice* case studies highlight typical challenges that teachers and students in the EAP classroom face. These examples can be used as means of comparison with your own teaching practices, and could also be used as discussion topics for teacher-training days.

Finally, each chapter ends with a bank of activities and worksheets relating to the theory covered in that chapter. There are more than 40 activities in total, providing you with a useful resource to help your students practise crucial skills.

The ideal way to approach this book as a reader is to start at the beginning and work your way through to the end. However, it is equally possible to dip into chapters that are more relevant to you and jump back to references in other chapters. Nor is it necessary to read all of the theory before using the activities – you may want to start with the activities and then read the input at the beginning of the chapter. After reading the practical theory at the beginning of the chapter, you may want to go back to the activities again and use them differently. Feel free to adapt the activities in any way that you feel works for your own situation – they are not cast in iron, never to be changed. You may find that by adding to them and adapting them that you come up with something much more suitable to your needs, so treat them as fluid entities.

Of the two skills – writing and reading – that this book deals with, we have focused primarily on the former, as we feel that for most students – and hence teachers – writing requires more input.

We hope that you will find this book a practical and enduring companion when teaching in the EAP classroom.

Acknowledgements

We would like to thank Dr Margot Blythman, Martin Harrison, Ermias Lakee, Iuri Monastirni, Karen Peter, Wilonja Mutebwe, Marta Pisanu, Professor Stephen Smith, Jonathan Spiers, Barbara Stewart, Phil Vellender, Professor John Flowerdew, Liz Hunt and many groups of students over the years.

We would like to say a special thank you to Anna Cowper, and also Jo Kent for her patience and expertise.

Sam McCarter and Phil Jakes

March 2009

1 Writing and reading approaches

What is English for Academic Purposes?

This book provides practical guidance and background theory for teachers of English for Academic Purposes (EAP). EAP is the English that is taught to second-/third-language students preparing to enter undergraduate and postgraduate courses at universities and other institutions of higher education. However, students may also be studying EAP at tertiary level, at high-school level, at technical colleges or at private language schools. Equally, they may already be studying an academic course in further/higher education and receiving additional language support.

The writing and reading you teach needs to fit the academic purposes of your students. You may, for example, find yourself:

- just starting a course in the new academic year;
- carrying out a needs-analysis to evaluate your students' competence in English;
- carrying out a needs-analysis to find out what students want/need to learn;
- easing students into the programme;
- demystifying academic writing/reading assignments, like reports and argument essays;
- teaching students to think, write and read critically, to read at speed and to do research.

It is this focus on preparing students for the specific academic requirements of English for higher education that distinguishes EAP from general English Language Teaching (ELT).

If you have come from an ELT background and have been thrown in at the deep end to teach EAP, the task ahead of you might seem daunting, if not impossible. The tips and guidance in this book, however, will help make the way clear for you, whether you follow the book through from beginning to end or dip into it at random.

Mastering writing and reading skills

In EAP, you may be teaching students who are preparing to study or who are already studying subjects like business, sociology, law, finance, science or the arts. As a language teacher, you will have to learn the types of writing and reading assignments that are common to the particular subject areas of your students. You need to familiarize yourself with the particular ways your students have to write and the particular texts they have to read. At the same time, however, the skills you already have as a more general language teacher are still highly relevant. Teaching

EAP is not about replacing the skills you already have, but about supplementing them so that you become a better all-round teacher.

In an EAP class, the language you are required to teach may be very varied, but it will change little over a short space of time. However, the various disciplines that your students study are subject to constant change. They are influenced by social developments, new laws, rules and regulations, and technology like the Internet. Part of your function as an EAP teacher is, therefore, to keep yourself up-to-date with any changes that affect your students.

For your EAP students, studying in English can seem complex, mysterious and fragmented. They may feel as if they are having to readjust their world and build completely new thinking processes and structures from scratch. And you may initially feel the same. However daunting and stifling all this may seem, mastery of the various systems can foster and develop freedom and creativity.

Within the discipline or specialist subject area

Whether you are working as a general EAP lecturer or within a particular department or subject like law or business, you may face greater demands both in terms of time and energy. You will need not only to gain knowledge and experience of the specific writing and reading assignments in EAP, but also to build knowledge of one or more subject areas, quite quickly.

The essential skills needed by the lecturer are the same as those for more general EAP, but with certain specific demands. A straw poll suggests that at the outset, a minimum of three hours of preparation time for a one-hour lesson would not be outrageous. It is also worth remembering that no matter how proficient you become, you cannot be a subject specialist. There is no harm therefore in admitting to your students that you do not know the answer to a problem. Equally, you need to remind your students that you are not a subject specialist and that they must check specialist conventions/procedures for validity, updates and changes to practice. For more on this, see Chapter 10.

Student expectations

To your students, and perhaps to you as an EAP teacher, the assignments your students are given in their field of study can seem vague, even obscure. As a first step, it is important to know what your students want from a language course, and for them to have an understanding of what skills they will need in order to operate efficiently and effectively.

If native speakers take time to acclimatize to their chosen subject, then is it not safe to assume that second-language speakers will face the same or even greater difficulties? This begs the question as to how effectively they can ever acclimatize.

A needs-analysis of your students is vital before any course as it can help you find out:

- what students need and what they want;
- where they are, from the point of view of language, eg, grammar, vocabulary, spelling and so on;
- what language skills they possess;
- what social/interactive skills they have;
- how emotionally mature they are as regards learning;
- if they have a capacity for independent learning;
- how motivated they are;
- how realistic their assessment of their own abilities is;
- whether they are open to change and development.

Students will also benefit from a needs-analysis in that it helps to focus them on their purpose for attending the EAP class. But most importantly their general effectiveness on your course will stem from their being able to see clearly the difference between what they want and what they actually need. A needs-analysis will also help narrow the language-learning path for your students and make it less ambiguous.

As your students learn and develop, their skills, needs and aspirations will change. A needs-analysis as an exercise is therefore not just essential at the beginning of a course. It needs to be revisited throughout any programme so that your students and you yourself can monitor progress.

With increasing student numbers and the time constraints faced by language tutors, a detailed needs-analysis is not always realistic. So you could make the analysis part of an interview with an assessment test, but it may have greater impact as a language exercise within the classroom, rather than as a bureaucratic exercise that can be kept in students' folders. See the needs-analysis questionnaire on page 12 and Activity 1.1 on page 21.

To make the needs-analysis into a reading exercise, give students a checklist syllabus for general English (see page 24), a skills audit for writing (see page 17) and a skills audit for reading (see page 18). Ask your students to complete the checklists before they start a course or as part of a homework exercise before a lecture/seminar. To simplify the activity, ask them to tick only the most important items in each document. See Activity 1.3 to encourage students to become more involved from the outset in the syllabus and what they are learning.

Needs-analysis/assessment questionnaire

Name: _____   Date: _____

Use the appropriate skills audit to help you answer the questions.

1   Why do you want to study English/EAP?

2   Which general skills do you hope to develop:

    writing/reading/speaking/listening?

3   Are there any particular skills that you want to learn or improve?

4   Are there any particular areas of language you want to improve?

Strengths and weaknesses

Tick and date the skills list.

5   What do you think are your main strengths in writing?

6   What do you think are your main strengths in reading?

7   What do you think are your main weaknesses in writing?

8   What do you think are your main weaknesses in reading?

Past experience of learning English

9   How were you taught English initially?

10 How would you describe your learning style?

11 Where do you think you will be six months/one year from now?

12 Are you aware of any major differences in academic language in English
    and your own language?

The needs-analysis can then be referred to and updated as students progress through any course. The checklists in the skills and audits act a record of where the students are. They also build confidence as it is easy for students to lose track of where they have journeyed from, especially when they feel weighed down by their studies or are immersed in the depths of a heavy assignment. The needs-analysis can also help you shape your lessons, which is why it needs to be an integral part of your planning.

Culture and text: Contrastive rhetoric

If we use a student-centred approach to writing and reading in EAP, contrasting the way texts in English are organized with that of other languages, eg, Arabic, Bantu, Bengali, Chinese, Japanese, Urdu, Yoruba, can provide you with some insight into your students' writing and reading. You may then over time be able to identify any problems that certain students may face. This area of study, known as contrastive rhetoric, compares texts or discourse across different languages/cultures to find differences or similarities. R. B. Kaplan (1966) represented the organization of paragraphs in a diagrammatic form, which is now not generally recognized – including by Kaplan himself – as being feasible:

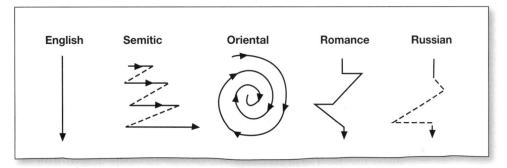

The diagram suggests that English is vertical, Romance languages are indirect and oriental languages are circular. Some people find these diagrams useful as a means of interpreting generally how different languages organize text, but they do have serious flaws. Is it possible to put all oriental languages under one diagram? Speakers of Urdu, for example, may see the way ideas are organized in their own language as vertical, and English as circular.

It is probably *not* possible to reduce the organization of text to diagrams such as those above. But students and teachers may seek to represent the structure of text in their own languages visually. Awareness of differences and similarities in writing and reading texts between a student's own language and English at a word, paragraph and article level can only help your teaching. It is also about becoming more acquainted with where the students are coming from and not just about trying to 'convert' your students without thinking about their backgrounds. The following exchange between an Arab/Kurdish-speaking postgraduate student and an EAP teacher illustrates this point. The teacher was asking the student about how he approaches writing a basic argument paragraph:

Teacher: *How do you do this in your own language?*

Student: [looking puzzled, laughing] *We don't.*

On further questioning, the student revealed that as an undergraduate he had never written an argument essay in his own language, and that students did not organize or question information in this way. Instead, they reproduced facts. A discussion ensued about how things are done in different languages/cultures. Highlighting students' language/cultural background in this way is not just about motivating students – it is about using and developing a practical tool that helps you ascertain learning differences and similarities. In the end, it may just be that the teacher is explaining a type of task like a particular genre of writing (see Chapter 4) in a way which is counterintuitive to the student. Awareness makes students feel valued. As part of a needs-analysis exercise, you could ask your students in groups to identify what they see as the three main differences and similarities between writing and reading texts in English and in their own languages. If you are teaching a multilingual class, you can put all the speakers of the same language together, or have a random mix. This can also help make your students more tolerant of each other as they become aware of how things are dealt with in different languages. You could do this activity at various stages throughout a course, but especially at the end, to see if your students' views have changed.

If you have a multilingual group, a variation of the above activity is to ask your students to bring in an example of a short text – one page maximum – on a topical subject in their own language. You can arrange them in groups, then ask them to explain to each other what the text is about and how the information is organized. Then, as described above, ask them to describe similarities and differences between the texts. You could then ask your students to draw a diagrammatic representation of the text (see Activity 5.4 and the related worksheet in Chapter 5, pages 91 and 92). This visual approach can help not just those of your students who have a visual approach to learning, but may also benefit those with other learning styles.

Learning styles and methodology

The way your students have been taught previously will influence how they learn. Your students, like you, will have their own individual learning styles. Some may respond better to visual input, some to verbal, some will need to use grammar or vocabulary in some way in order to activate it, some will need to write everything down and others will need to learn it by heart. Some may like learning in groups and some may prefer to work on their own.

The teaching methods that your students are used to in other situations may be at variance with the styles in the modern EAP classroom. Students may come from educational traditions where information is presented not to be challenged but to be absorbed. There may then be a mismatch between what your students perceive as learning and your views and practice, which could result in conflict. Hence the importance of knowing even a little bit about your students' backgrounds.

Finding out about what approach(es) your students prefer to use or are used to in an initial assessment will help you to design your course and develop your teaching. This may challenge your own assumptions about how students learn and could help you to be more flexible and accommodating, while still maintaining control. For example, you may have to work on easing some students into groupwork or pairwork; or focus them on concentrating on the teacher. You may need to learn to vary the activities in a smooth way, and you may find that you have to develop new learning styles and/or challenge old ones.

Learning styles can form the basis of an ongoing discussion with students both during and at the end of a course. Your students could be asked to discuss whether their learning styles have changed, and how and whether they feel the change has helped them. A debriefing questionnaire can be used at the end of the course to evaluate the methodology and not just the content of your course.

Writing and reading approaches: Bottom-up and top-down

Some students may favour a bottom-up approach to writing and reading, manipulating discrete language items and small chunks of language to create the bigger picture. Others may be more comfortable with a top-down approach using meta-cognitive skills: predicting the content of a text, identifying the organization of a text and common text relationships like problem, cause, solution; or condition proposal, result and so on. Have you considered your own approach? Is it consistent? Or even should it be? You may find in your own teaching style that you favour a bottom-up approach to writing, but the reverse in reading, or vice versa. There may also be occasions where you move up and down the scale from bottom to top and top to bottom. For more on this, see Chapter 8.

The predominant approach in any institution may be bottom-up, but you may find that EAP is more inclined to the top-down approach, with the development of an ability to think critically. But the grammar must not be forgotten. See Good practice 1.2 and Activity 1.2.

Teacher expectations

How writing and reading fit into the students' subject areas needs to be made clear at the outset. Otherwise, fragmentation of what is demanded of them in terms of skills and knowledge, especially with regard to the various writing/reading tasks, will stop your students acquiring an overview of the course. The syllabus and skills audits mentioned above help in developing course design, determining what has been done, what is to be done and what needs to be revisited in order to address gaps in students' knowledge. More importantly, they set out for your students what is expected of them.

Treating the syllabus as a living, organic document and allowing it to be adapted means your students can 'own' the document along with you and your institution. See Activity 1.3. By involving the students, even just in analysing the syllabus, you can find out how much importance they attach to discrete items. With the syllabus in their files/portfolios or saved electronically, students can use it to keep a record of what they have done by numbering each item in sequence as they master it, thus encouraging them to map the course they are following. By building their own picture of the language it will help foster independent learning, thereby strengthening study skills.

Skills for effective writing and reading

Student: *I can't write according to a model/template.*

Student: *I can't scan. I have to read.*

Your students will present with a jagged profile: they may be very good at speaking, but very poor at writing, or vice versa. This may also be the case across writing and reading genres and study skills. Assumptions about a student's competence in writing based on previous academic experience have to be treated with care. The student who excels in one genre, such as describing a process, may fail miserably in producing an argumentative essay. Similarly, the student who is good at writing a short analytical text may baulk at a longer essay. Skills proficiency, like any ability, can atrophy if not utilized. The skills your students need have to be revisited, thought about and discussed – not merely listed.

A skills audit of your students at the beginning of the course and then at various stages throughout is useful not just to identify strengths and weaknesses, but also any developments.

At a later date when your students have mastered a number of the skills, you can ask them to classify the skills into macro and micro skills. This serves as revision and is also a confidence-building exercise.

Getting to know your students

Apart from carrying out a needs-analysis to find out how much our students know, as teachers we also need to show the students themselves how much they know and what is expected of them. One way of doing this is to throw them in at the deep end and give them a writing exercise or a reading task, without providing any help. This might work with some classes and/or students, but easing them in gently to your own way of doing things will help you and your students. For an activity to ease your students into a top-down approach to reading, see Activity 1.2.

You can also give your students a questionnaire on getting to know each other that can be found in many coursebooks, or you could ask them to prepare a short talk about their proposed future studies. This will give you an insight into your students, their expectations and ambitions. See Activity 1.4.

Many of the writing and reading activities in this book involve oral preparation and lots of discussion, which we strongly recommend as a means of reinforcing and expanding your students' skills in these two areas. The same applies to listening.

Writing skills audit

Name: _____   Date: _____

Tick the appropriate column.

		strength	weakness
1	planning	☐	☐
2	creating/generating ideas	☐	☐
3	organizing/categorizing ideas	☐	☐
4	ranking ideas according to importance	☐	☐
5	linking ideas	☐	☐
6	writing introductions	☐	☐
7	organizing a paragraph	☐	☐
8	paraphrasing	☐	☐
9	summarizing	☐	☐
10	describing a process	☐	☐
11	writing an argument	☐	☐
12	writing an explanation	☐	☐
13	writing thesis statements/scope statements	☐	☐
14	describing cause-and-effect relationships	☐	☐
15	thinking critically	☐	☐
16	identifying and writing about problems/solutions	☐	☐
17	writing topic statements	☐	☐
18	following a particular genre of writing	☐	☐
19	writing for a purpose	☐	☐
20	referencing within a text	☐	☐
21	comparing and contrasting	☐	☐
22	writing with accuracy	☐	☐
23	writing conclusions	☐	☐
24	drawing inferences	☐	☐
25	handling different sources of information/data	☐	☐
26	drafting and revising	☐	☐

Reading skills audit

Name: _____   Date: _____

Tick the appropriate column.

		strength	weakness
1	activating a schema/schemata*	☐	☐
2	skimming	☐	☐
3	scanning	☐	☐
4	predicting	☐	☐
5	reading fast	☐	☐
6	reading under pressure	☐	☐
7	understanding gist	☐	☐
8	referring to several sources simultaneously	☐	☐
9	understanding a whole text	☐	☐
10	extracting meaning from a paragraph	☐	☐
11	answering questions about a discrete part of a text	☐	☐
12	reading for leisure/pleasure	☐	☐
13	juggling information	☐	☐
14	evaluating as you read	☐	☐
15	reading without translating	☐	☐
16	answering comprehension questions	☐	☐
17	drawing conclusions	☐	☐
18	making assumptions	☐	☐
19	drawing inferences	☐	☐
20	evaluating critically	☐	☐

*a picture/image or sequence of images that are produced as you read, by drawing on previous knowledge/experience

Good practice 1.1

The importance of student background knowledge

Dmitri, in his mid-twenties, is currently applying to do a business course in economics, finance and management at a British university and has just received his first conditional offer.

He has a professional family background – both his parents are university graduates, one a mechanical engineer and the other a doctor. Following in his father's footsteps, Dmitri took a five-year degree course in mechanical engineering at a Moldovan university. He describes the course as being mainly factual and mathematical, with exams each term testing factual information by completing gaps and solving mathematical/statistical problems. Reading formed part of the course, but there was not much writing, except for a long essay towards the end. This essay required some basic critical thinking, comparing factual knowledge, but not much evaluation.

One term of the course was spent in the UK at an agricultural college. Dmitri enjoyed it tremendously, but as his English was not very good he could not follow the theory. However, he was able to cope with the more practical components, which took place mainly on a farm. This gave him a taste for life in the United Kingdom, where he is now living.

His change of direction from one subject to another – mechanical engineering to business management – does not daunt him. Instead, Dmitri feels that his former training as an engineer has equipped him with a solid grounding in statistical research, detailed planning, critical analysis and logical conclusions based on scientific observation rather than speculative theory.

Now studying and working in London, Dmitri appears to be very goal-orientated and does not seem easily distracted from his course of action. He has devoted himself to acquiring skills he perceives as relevant to his aims, investing a lot of time and energy.

He is currently working in restaurant management in London whilst following an English language course and taking additional private English lessons. He is also studying for the European Computer Driving Licence, hoping to pass all stages before commencing university in September. On top of this, Dmitri is taking a certificate in business administration at a local college. For this he has to write seven 300-word essays in English, each on different aspects of business management: working effectively with others, planning, setting out and meeting objectives, aspects of self-management, etc. The course is computer-based, involving Internet research.

As he has completed a degree in his own language, Dmitri feels that he should be able to obtain a degree provided he can achieve the right level of English. As a further step towards this aim he speaks only English with his flatmates, so that everything he does appears to be designed to build and activate a sequence of schemata in preparation for his studies.

Asked what approach he likes to take when studying, Dmitri stated that he preferred to see things globally and to understand the detail afterwards, rather than the other way round. He thinks writing is his weakness, and possibly also reading. When planning and studying, he likes to take a vertical approach, seeing things as a sequence of steps in an orderly fashion. Being highly motivated and goal-orientated with a very flexible and dynamic approach to learning, he has planned the best way of achieving a British degree. Finding out about Dmitri's background, abilities and goals (see Activities 1.1 to 1.4) helped Dmitri's teacher cater for his needs. The teacher was then able to steer him towards his new-found aims of studying economics and setting up his own business. It was obvious that Dmitri needed little help with approaching learning globally, or motivation. It meant that his not inconsiderable skills could be used to improve his writing skills. Activities 1.1 to 1.4 also helped Dmitri see what stage he was at language-wise and skills-wise. Within a normal class setting, the teacher could manipulate tasks so that an individual student's demands could be catered for: having one group focusing on grammar, another on spelling, another on linking, but all essentially involved in the same task. As regards time management, this assisted the teacher by allowing him to deal with a range of students and their needs. The secret was knowing even a little background information, which saved time all round.

Good practice 1.2

Using learning skills to help you as a teacher

Jane is an English teacher from the UK who has done an undergraduate degree in English and drama at an English university, followed by a conversion degree in psychology and then an MSc in forensic psychology.

She is a highly efficient learner who describes her learning style as kinesthetic, which on reflection she links to her drama course. Her method of preparing for exams is choosing the most likely subjects that she can do with ease and breaking them down into manageable chunks of no more than eight cards for each subject/topic, with the information written as bullet points. This stage of the process takes place in the library and once it is complete, Jane then has to rehearse the information aloud, walking around her flat until she knows the information completely.

Jane feels this learning process has changed over time, moving away from reliance on the physical rehearsing of the information she needs to learn to a more visual approach.

She noted that initially, the demands of an academic course were great, but with each subsequent course it became easier. She also pointed out that what was being demanded in writing from students changed over time. In her first degree, writing involved continuous text with few sub-headings, whereas on her latest course more sub-headings were required. Regarding task types, Jane felt she was better at writing longer essays than set assignments that were expected to be written according to a template.

Pre-university, Jane was assessed as not capable of achieving a high grade at university. In fact, she achieved a first-class honours for her first two degrees and a distinction for her MSc. Now a teacher herself, Jane puts the method of learning she used as a student to good use when preparing her lessons as an English language teacher, and in her presentations when working as a trainer. Her awareness of her own style of learning through a range of courses has given her additional insight into how her learners learn. It has also now led Jane into training teachers herself. Her teaching style is very much like that of Dmitri's teacher.

Activity 1.1

Reading, thinking and writing

Aims:

- to help students evaluate their own career and put it into perspective
- to help students organize information and identify elements of a particular type of writing

Materials:

- a copy of **Good practice 1.1**
- a copy of the needs-analysis questionnaire

Level: Intermediate/B1 to Advanced/C1

Time: 45 minutes

Methodology

1 Inform students that they are going to write up a case study about a partner.
2 Give students a copy of the materials above.
3 Ask students to read **Good practice 1.1**.
4 Ask students to identify a certain number of language features in the **Good practice**, eg, tenses, linking devices, organization, use of passives, type of vocabulary and structure of the text (ie, chronological, descriptive or argumentative). Choose no more than three of these features.
5 Ask students to look at the needs-analysis questionnaire. Ask them to decide which questions, if any, from the needs-analysis questionnaire were asked by the teacher to ascertain the information relating to the student in **Good practice 1.1.**
6 Ask each student to choose and mark between five and seven questions that they feel comfortable answering on the questionnaire. Ask them to give the questionnaire to a partner, who will ask the questions and follow up as necessary. While asking the questions, the partner should take clear notes.
7 When both members of the pair have made notes, they should write up their own case study about their partner, using the features they identified in step 5. This can be done in class or for homework. Before the case study is handed in for correction, each student should check that the information provided reflects what their partner said.
8 Ask students if you can keep copies of the texts as anonymous samples to create a bank of writing materials.

Follow-up 1: If acceptable to you, allow your students to interview you about your approach to learning and any difficulties you have faced. If you do not wish to give too much away, at least reveal the essentials – your educational background, for example. This process helps build trust.

Follow-up 2: Repeat the task using **Good practice 1.2**.

Activity 1.2

Raising awareness of what students know

Aims:

- to ease your students into prediction in reading
- to help students predict information and follow clearly the thread/development of a text

Materials:

- the title of a reading passage
- any sub-headings from the reading passage, or a list of jumbled or unjumbled paragraph headings from the passage
- comprehension questions
- the reading passage

Level: Intermediate/B1 to Advanced/C1

Time: 30 minutes

Methodology

1 Ask students to work in groups of three or four. Give students the title of the reading passage. Ask them to make a list of information they would expect to see in an article with this title. Then ask them to think about how the text might be organized: problem/solution, cause/effect, chronological development, etc. Give a time limit of five to ten minutes and ask for seven possible pieces of information.

2 Give students the sub-headings or paragraph headings. Ask them to refine their predictions about the text content and add any further information.

3 Give students the comprehension questions. Again, ask students to refine their predictions and add any further information to their original list. Point out how the questions themselves are a type of summary of the text – they guide the reader.

4 Give students the reading passage and ask them to answer the comprehension questions.

5 When you have checked the answers with the whole class, ask students to explain the importance of placing a reading text within a schema, and to explain the process of prediction.

Follow-up 1: Reading

In subsequent reading exercises, you can follow the same procedure or reduce the stages by giving the title, sub-headings and questions all together, until you think students are beginning to predict the passage contents unprompted.

Follow-up 2: Writing

Give students a writing exercise with a similar organizational principle (eg, cause/effect). Before they begin writing, ask them to mine the reading text for verbs, sentence structures, linking devices and general nouns. You can ask students to focus on one, two or more of these.

Activity 1.3

The syllabus, the skills audit, the students

Aim: to help students become more aware of what they are learning

Materials:

- a Writing or Reading skills audit questionnaire
- an extract from a language syllabus or for more advanced students the whole syllabus
- worksheet (see page 24)

Level: Intermediate/B1 to Advanced/C1

Time: 30 minutes

Methodology

1 Give students the materials above – either the skills audit photocopiables on pages 17 and 18 *or* a whole syllabus.
2 Ask students to work either individually, in pairs or groups and decide what they think are the most important points that should be covered in the course. Ask them to limit their choices to seven or two or three per page.
3 Ask them to grade the items on the list in the skills audit or the syllabus 1–7, where 1 is the most important.
4 Allow variation within each pair/group, but encourage them to justify their choices for the benefit of themselves and language learning generally.
5 Ask students to give you feedback. If you have an interactive whiteboard, you can enter agreed choices on a master document.
6 You may want to do a repeat exercise at different stages during the course.
7 Give students your choices and discuss why you have chosen them.
8 Encourage students to ask you to cover items in the course and negotiate with them what should and should not be included in your teaching.

Activity 1.4

Finding out about each other

Aim: to help students organize information and gain an overview of their studies

Materials: a computer/interactive whiteboard

Level: Intermediate/B1 to Advanced/C1

Time: 45 minutes or more, depending on the number of students

Methodology

1 Ask students to work in groups of four and prepare a mini-presentation of their proposed course(s) of study. Tell them the presentation should last no longer than five minutes, with time for questions.
2 Ask students to plan a series of slides to present using PowerPoint™, or on the interactive whiteboard.
3 Tell students they are limited to between five and seven slides, so that they are encouraged to summarize their information.
4 Ask them to give information about the course content, types of writing assignment, and why they want to do the course.
5 Set a time limit for preparation of 20 to 30 minutes. You could also set this as a homework task.
6 Give the students 10 minutes to practise giving the presentation to each other.
7 Ask each group to make a presentation to the class, with each member of the group contributing.

Worksheet: Activity 1.3

Syllabus/Skills worksheet

Rank as many items as you can 1–7, where 1 is most important and 7 is not so important. Then choose at least three items below which you think need to be included in your course.

		Writing	**Reading**
1	thinking critically		
2	cohesion		
3	coherence		
4	pronouns		
5	word order		
6	simple connections		
7	complex sentences		
8	thesis statements		
9	generalizations		
10	purpose		
11	referencing		
12	addition		
13	result		
14	conclusion		
15	concession		
16	summary		
17	exemplification		
18	comparison		
19	clarification		
20	reservation		
21	cause/effect		
22	problem/solution		
23	doubt		
24	certainty		

2 Understanding task questions and selecting ideas

When writing and reading for academic purposes, your students will need to understand a wide range of questions relating to different tasks. The aim of this chapter is to help you guide your students in both skills by highlighting the relationship between them, so that they are totally flexible in both and their approach to writing evolves beyond the purely mechanical.

This flexibility helps take away some of the fear that can accompany writing, and can even make it pleasurable. The steps described below may be absorbed or adapted and/or improved by your more able students to suit their particular needs. For the less competent among your students, the guidelines can act as a standard for measuring themselves against.

Steps in the writing process

The writing process involves a series of steps, starting from an exploration and analysis of the essay question. Then comes the generation and organization of ideas, followed by the physical acts of writing and critical thinking (see Chapter 5 for more on critical thinking). The latter stages, which are dealt with in subsequent chapters, include selecting types of text and redrafting.

If we start with a general writing assignment like an essay question, the first step is teaching your students how to look at the question. To help analyse the question, it can be broken up into manageable chunks. Students will then be less inclined to jump into the physical act of writing before they think about what exactly they are going to write.

The topic or subject of a task

Questions obviously vary – in type according to the task and in complexity according to the level of the students. Nevertheless, the principles of organization are the same whether at a whole-text level, at a paragraph level or at a sentence level. However, specific assignments may allow for features like bullet points and numbered text, which might not be appropriate elsewhere.

Let us take the following essay title as an example:

The incidence of crime in many countries is increasing. Analyse/Discuss the impact of technology on both facilitating and solving crime.

In the first sentence, we can see that the more general topic is *the incidence of crime … is increasing*; while in the second sentence it is clear that the topic is narrowed to make it easier to write about: *the impact of technology on both facilitating and solving crime.*

Questions to ask before writing

Asking questions at each step of the writing process will help develop your students' thinking skills and will guide them right from the planning stage to the final draft. For an essay question, students can ask themselves the following questions:

Purpose:	Why am I writing this essay?
Topic:	What is the topic or subject of this essay?
Target:	Who am I writing it for?
Organization:	How am I going to organize this essay?
Thesis:	What is the thesis of this essay and how am I going to state it?

As a warm-up to an initial writing task, you could also:

- ask students to number the questions in the box above and match them to the relevant parts of the essay question;
- break up the essay task into its different components and then have students form questions to ask themselves in order to analyse the essay question (in this case the questions above could be given afterwards);
- use the questions as the basis of an oral explanation of the essay question by more advanced students, who might want to present a detailed analysis to the whole class or to groups (the class can then choose the best interpretation and write it down);
- encourage students to use the questions as a guide in order to rewrite the essay question in their own words (again, the class can choose the best interpretation).

In subsequent lessons, the questions above can be put on the board as a reminder for students.

Target audience

Getting to grips with the target audience of a writing task is an essential element of writing, as it helps to get your students thinking about what they need to write. The relative importance of the questions in the box above will be determined by the situation in which the writing task takes place. For example, for an essay set by an EAP teacher, the target audience is obviously the teacher. However, for an essay set by a university lecturer in a particular subject, perhaps as part of an assignment which counts towards a degree, the target audience will be the lecturer, who will be assessing the work primarily from the subject point of view. This is likely to affect the student's approach to the task. And so the target audience of the task needs to be expressed in the general terms of practising towards similar tasks on a university course.

The earlier students understand the place of the writing tasks in their subject of study, the easier it will be to explain the relevance of each writing task and to motivate and interest your students. For further practice in the terminology used in questions, see Activity 2.3 and the worksheet for this chapter on pages 37 and 39 respectively.

Purpose in writing

Student: *What's the point of doing this writing exercise?*

Another crucial guiding mechanism for your students in writing is understanding the purpose of any task. Students can be asked to express the purpose of the task in their own words using a purpose clause:

We are doing this task in order to …

Before beginning any writing task, you can give your students several different texts and ask them to select the purpose for each one from a list (see Activity 2.2). When they are more proficient, they can identify the purpose themselves without referring to the list. Systematic exposure to more and more tasks, as well as a variety of tasks, will help your students build their own picture of what the purpose is of writing and reading texts in their subject.

Topic and organization

Apart from the subject of the essay, your students need to develop an appreciation of organization in writing. In other words, they need to be shown how a question can require the discussion points within an essay to be organized in a particular way. Let us look at the previous essay question again as an example:

The incidence of crime in many countries is increasing. Analyse/Discuss the impact of technology on both facilitating and solving crime.

From this essay question we could draw up the following rough organization:

- an increase in crime (problem)
- only discuss technology's impact on crime (cause/factor), ie, makes crime easier (problems/effects) helps solve crime (solutions)

The pie chart on the next page can help students to see that they do not have to write about all aspects of a topic. For the essay question above, only the elements with asterisks against them relate to the writing task. Over a period of time, you could make your own checklist of the main elements that make up an essay question and ask students to use it to select what they are going to write about. For a description of how essays are organized, see Chapter 3.

Elements of essay questions

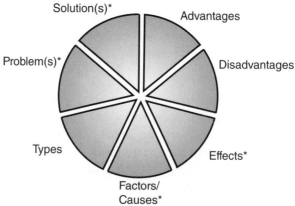

*elements that relate to the example writing task

Figure 2.1: Pie chart showing what different elements a student would be expected to cover based on the essay question about crime.

Analysing task questions like this is a complex skill. In order to appreciate the difficulty students might face, it is useful to try to create your own questions. Aim to write the questions in such a way that the student should include at least three elements in his/her essay. The process is the reverse of that described above. Start with the elements in the pie chart and build up different questions about crime or other general subjects.

If your students are of a sufficiently high level, question creation can be demonstrated to them. You can then ask them to create their own questions from a set of prompt words, eg,

globalization – benefits – drawbacks/damage – future

The level of difficulty can be varied by dictating how many parts of the pie chart above they need to use (at least two, three, etc.). This will help students better understand the structure of questions. For further practice see Activity 2.3 and the worksheet on pages 37 and 39.

Understanding terminology in questions

Student: *I understand the subject, but I don't know what I have to do.*

Another feature of academic essay questions that determines how your students organize their essays is specific nouns and verbs used in the essay questions. These nouns and verbs are intended to guide the students as they write, eg,

*What are the **benefits** of ...?*

*What are the **advantages** and **disadvantages** of ...?*

*What are the **causes**, **effects** and **solutions** of ...?*

While nouns like this are relatively easy to deal with, verbs like the following can cause greater ambiguity: *analyse, argue, classify, demonstrate, describe, differentiate, discuss, evaluate, examine, explain, identify, outline* and *produce*. It is these nouns and verbs that help students to state the thesis and structure the organization of an assignment.

An essay question could contain just one verb, or two or more. When you introduce students to the verbs above in essay questions, there is a good chance that your students will have been exposed to some of the words before and will want clarification, especially as to the difference between *argue* and *discuss* and *analyse* and *evaluate*.

To make these words less ambiguous, you can give students:

- the list of verbs and ask them to explain the meaning in their own words, with or without the help of a dictionary. The verbs you give will obviously depend on the level of the class and what they can cope with. Seven or eight words would be sufficient;
- the verbs and their meanings (on separate pieces of paper) and ask them to match them;
- the meanings of some of the verbs and ask them to give the meanings of the remaining verbs in their own words;
- the meanings only and ask them to supply the verbs as best they can. Then give them the list of verbs to complete the exercise;
- a list of topics and verbs and ask them to build their own questions (see Activity 2.3).

See Chapter 3 for the different text types which these organizing words relate to and how they can be used to guide the organization of a piece of writing.

Creating ideas

Teacher: *I have a 19-year-old Spanish student who has difficulty coming up with ideas.*

A common and easy way to help students generate ideas and prepare for writing is to use brainstorming activities. Brainstorming works well when students:

- do not exclude any information whatsoever;
- use a blank sheet of paper with the main idea in note form written in the centre with or without the circles (see Figure 2.2 on page 30);
- make sure there is a lot of empty space;
- write ideas that come into their heads in random order;

- write short notes or content words/collocations;
- do not try to put their ideas in any order or hierarchy.

Let us take our example question again:

The incidence of crime in many countries is increasing. Analyse/Discuss the impact of technology on both facilitating and solving crime.

At this stage it would be better to write only *crime (rates) increasing* in the centre and then deal with the narrower elements of the question later.

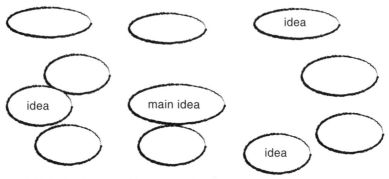

Figure 2.2: Brainstorming map with no connecting lines.

With students who are more visually orientated, you could use a selection of images to help trigger ideas. If students have access to the Internet, they can search for images and write down at random what they see.

Students can be put into groups and each group given a different visual source to generate ideas. Groups then keep notes of their ideas using different media, including electronic formats (podcasts/digital pictures/sound recordings) and paper-based formats (graphs, charts, pictures or words). Once each group has come up with some ideas, all the ideas can be collated as a whole-class activity.

For students who have difficulty dealing with conceptual ideas on the spot in brainstorming, a simple word-association exercise may work: *crime, criminal, hurt, society, punishment, cost, offend, judge, court,* etc. Once your students have done this, have them compare their words and then write a master list on the board. You can also make your own list and show this to your students at the end of the exercise to see whether the lists are similar. If students do not have a wide vocabulary, this process allows students to make note of an idea briefly which can then be expanded on afterwards: *credit card fraud, credit card theft, identity theft, worldwide network* . The words do not have to be nouns or phrases; they can be single adjectives or verbs. This allows students to catch feelings and thoughts that flash through their minds and which are difficult to immediately express or summarize in a phrase.

For students who like to see things as part of a whole, *if* chains or cause-and-effect chains are useful to trigger simple ideas (see Good practice 2.1 and Activity 2.4).

If you want a very controlled activity to help students focus on producing ideas for pre-reading and writing, give your students a reading passage heading and paragraph headings. Then ask them to generate ideas. In this way you can relate idea creation and organization to reading and writing and motivate students to think for themselves (see Activity 2.1).

If your students find it difficult to juggle two ideas and combine them in subordinating or coordinating clauses, assembling the ideas in the first place will require guidance. Constantly seek to find different ways to develop your own strategies to encourage your students to think about and create ideas.

Selecting ideas

The brainstorming diagram students produce can be used to help select ideas and then link and classify them. At this stage, ideas can be rejected, refined, adapted or added to. To give an idea room to develop, it can be transferred from the brainstorming sheet to a separate sheet and then other ideas from the brainstorming can be added to it. The idea can also be developed through word association, or by giving students ideas to blend with those they have collected.

A mini spidergram can be created for each separate idea, which can form a paragraph or a series of paragraphs.

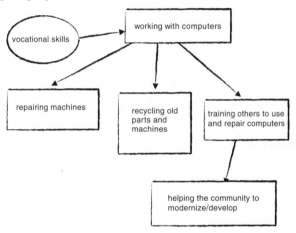

Figure 2.3: A spidergram showing how ideas can be related to one another to form the basis of a paragraph.

Showing students samples of previous brainstorming exercises you have done will help motivate them. A bank of laminated samples could be kept and given out to students at the beginning of or after a brainstorming activity, for discussion.

Where students need guidance in brainstorming, or if you want to introduce idea selection, a previous sample from a student can be used. Each idea could be written on a card and students could then attach them to a central idea. They then select which ideas they want to write about. The original may be given as a paper copy or put on the board.

Recycling ideas

Teacher: *You don't know that you know.*

You may find that your students need help to tap the knowledge that they already have, but are not aware of. One way to help students overcome the feeling that they do not have ideas is to show them that they do not know that they already have a wealth of ideas not just from the world around them, but from other essay questions and reading they have done in the past. It is easy for students to associate particular ideas with one essay question only. You can show your students that ideas, like words, can be used in a variety of essays and situations. If you take the theme of our previous example essay question on crime, one general solution to reducing crime rates might be education at secondary school. Education as a solution to a problem can apply in a wide range of situations: *prevent crime, reduce obesity, reduce vandalism, encourage sport, encourage respect, promote understanding of ecology, promote respect for the environment.*

Flexibility of this kind can easily be developed by providing several general solutions or specific solutions and then asking students to find situations where they would apply. Recycling ideas from previous exercises and general reading also applies to preparation for reading exercises and reading or studying in general.

Purpose, selecting ideas, topic and organization in reading

In helping students to read, the same principles described above apply. Brainstorming before writing is like predicting the content of a reading text using the title, sub-headings and perhaps comprehension questions (see Activity 2.1). Asking oneself what the purpose of a reading text is, who the target audience is, what the general topic is and what the organizing principles are, also applies.

A big difference is how your students find their way around a text written by someone else.

Reading techniques: skimming, scanning and studying

When preparing to write, students need to select discrete ideas to write about. When reading, students need to extract specific details or discrete information from a text, to understand gist or general information in a text. For the former, an ability to glide over the words without engaging in meaning is required. However, if students are used to 'studying' a text or have not been trained to scan, they will skim the text until they find the information. This in itself is no bad thing, but if speed is required it is better to look for a 'word picture' from the bottom of a paragraph upwards, or diagonally from bottom to top or left to right, right to left. If the lines of a text are long, students can scan a paragraph in a zigzag pattern from bottom left to a point at the top and then down and up again. Equally, they can start top left and scan again in a zigzag from top to bottom, and so on. More advanced students can be taught to jump around the paragraph or to look at the centre of a paragraph and use peripheral vision to look at different parts of the text. Which technique or combination of techniques students use is not important, but challenging their established ways of doing things will help create flexibility.

When skimming, it is important for students to start building a picture (see Chapter 8). The more proficient student will jump around the text looking at words that build themes and organization. Students who are used to reading and learning every word will need to learn to read only content words like nouns and verbs. The idea that reading is not about reading every word is a concept that students from many backgrounds and educational traditions may find difficult to accept. For more on reading, see Chapter 8.

Good practice 2.1

Helping students analyse questions and generate ideas

When dealing with writing tasks, the major problems faced by EAP teachers are getting students to understand the question, building students' confidence so that they can use the knowledge they already have, and creating new ideas.

Beatrice is a student who finds it difficult to analyse questions and then generate ideas, but once she has done this she can write competently.

A music teacher from Italy, Beatrice has a degree in musicology from an Italian conservatory. At university, Beatrice did not have to write any essays for her degree. Her exams were either practical or oral exams, for which she had to do a lot of reading. The aim of the exams was primarily to check factual information, with questions on the lives of particular composers and periods of music. She did not have to write any continuous prose.

While preparing for the oral exams, Beatrice and her fellow students worked together in self-help groups. After they had memorized the information, they practised saying it to each other, so that they would have a series of speeches in their heads. Beatrice commented that she did not think that this was a very effective way of learning as she quickly forgot the information that she had learnt.

Beatrice wants to do a Postgraduate Certificate in Education (PGCE) at London University. Like many students moving from one system to another, Beatrice finds the way of working at London University is totally different from what she was used to in Italy.

As she is working as a piano teacher, the language Beatrice is most familiar with is piano-related. She finds that she does not have the chance to develop other more general music vocabulary, nor more general or academic vocabulary.

Beatrice found the early stages of writing difficult: first understanding writing questions exactly, also interpreting any kind of data presented in graphic or pictorial form, and then generating ideas. In fact, she depended more on the teacher and other students for ideas than her own resources. Beatrice's level of English is advanced and her writing is fluent, well organized and contains few mistakes, but she cannot write without planning first.

Beatrice volunteered a possible reason for her inability to generate ideas. She described briefly an incident where she had to walk off stage at a concert because she could not perform. She can now only play with the music in front of her. She described her learning style as visual and practical, but she likes to memorize information.

Beatrice has adopted different techniques to overcome her problems. She took to the idea of brainstorming, which she had not done before. For her, brainstorming with a partner worked well, and talking through specific ideas helped put them in context. When faced with writing an impromptu text in a class test, and incidentally for discussions or oral exams, she really liked generating and developing ideas through word-association chains (see Activity 2.4). The reason she gave for this was that she could attach the ideas to words afterwards. She also said it helped her in developing her speaking.

Good practice 2.2

Honing organizational skills helps reduce writing errors

Tesfaye is a quiet but apparently confident student. He can understand reading texts readily and talk about answers to questions without much problem. However, on closer acquaintance there is a clear lack of ability to transfer skills from one type of task to another, eg, using his competence and confidence in reading to help him complete writing tasks.

Tesfaye is in his early twenties and is living in London. He is a second-language speaker of English. Amharic, which uses the Ge'ez alphabet, is his first language and he is generally competent in English.

He is following a one-year part-time foundation course in applied sciences at a further education institution, studying 10 hours per week. The purpose of doing the course is to enter university to take a scientific degree. The main mode of delivery of information on the course is lectures, with some practical experiment sessions.

The classes sometimes last three hours, but Tesfaye does not feel that he has any problem concentrating or listening for this length of time. Nor does he have problems studying scientific subjects in general, as he is familiar with the terminology.

The writing he does on his part-time course is mainly describing processes and writing evaluations of the experiments, which are of between 150 and 200 words in length. As the questions for his assignments are very clear and precise and as the answers can be written in part in bullet points, he finds the writing easy.

Despite the good grades he has received so far, he senses that he still needs help with his writing, especially in terms of grammar and style. Tesfaye would like to have specific feedback about these two areas. When asked about language support at his college, he said that there is nothing for part-time students with his background, adding that there is help for overseas students who are paying overseas fees, but he does not have any money to pay for the help.

It is clear from Tesfaye's writing in class that his problem lies with the limited nature of his exposure to writing tasks in an academic situation. When he is faced with writing tasks that require a much broader range of writing skills and knowledge, especially those outside the purely scientific field, he makes more mistakes.

Tesfaye benefited particularly from writing and reading tasks that improved his awareness of organization. He could complete exercises in matching headings and paragraphs easily, so it did not take long for him to transfer the concept to writing. Tasks like matching paragraph headings, which instil organizational skills, were useful pre-writing exercises for Tesfaye. They also work for many other students. This approach led to a reduction in mistakes in Tesfaye's writing, mainly because he did not have to think so much about the organization and could concentrate on the discrete items in writing like spelling and grammar (see Activities 2.1 and 2.2).

Activity 2.1

Introducing thinking to writing and reading

Aims:

- to help students see the relationship between writing and reading and to see where thinking fits in
- to help students use their own ideas in the writing/reading process
- to build students' confidence in their own knowledge and abilities
- to encourage students to think for themselves

Materials:

- a reading passage on a general academic subject (1 page/1.5 pages in length)
- the title of the passage
- a list of headings for paragraphs or sections
- a list of words or phrases from the reading passage
- a large flip chart page or a computer per group

Level: Intermediate/B1 to Advanced/C1
Time: 45 to 60 minutes

Methodology

1 Choose a fairly easy topical reading passage, eg, oil running out, investment in public services, population growth; which features a particular type of organization you want to focus on, eg, problem/solution or cause/effect.
2 Ask students to work in groups. Give them the materials as above, except for the reading passage.
3 Ask students to predict the content of the reading passage using the information that they have, their knowledge of the world and their imaginations. Ask them to write down their ideas on a large sheet of paper or on the computer. Later, a member of their group will present their ideas to the class.
4 Leave students to their own devices or give them guidance about organizing their information. They can use the organization they have employed in brainstorming techniques or word association/idea association techniques described previously.
5 Set a time limit and go around the class, encouraging students. Remind them of the time.
6 Working with the whole class, collate the information from each group representative.
7 When students have presented their ideas, and you have answered any questions, give them an essay question. This will help them organize the information they have.
8 After students have written the essay in class, give them the reading passage to read. Allow them to adapt their writing using information or phrases from the passage.
9 You may want to give the students reading comprehension questions relating to the passage.
10 Ask students to explain what effect the process had on their writing and also on their comprehension of the reading passage. Ask them to consider the thinking processes they used.

Activity 2.2

Reading for purpose: using samples/models for reading and writing

Aims:
- to help students identify text types
- to help build students' confidence in their writing and reading

Materials:
- sample writing assignment texts written by students illustrating evaluation, classification, etc.
- model texts from different sources
- a list of the purposes of each text, which is deliberately not entirely accurate
- topic ideas related to the texts
- an assignment question

Level: Intermediate/B1 to Advanced/C1

Time: 45 to 60 minutes

Methodology

1 Number the texts. Remove the assignment questions from the sample answers and the titles from the model texts.
2 Ask students to work in groups and tell them that they are going to analyse different types of writing, both sample and model texts. You only need a few samples of writing by former students, which you can use with their permission.
3 Give students the sample texts and ask them to decide what types of text they are and what the original essay question might have been. How many texts you give the students depends on the level of the class, what you are focusing on and how many types of text you have taught so far. You do not need to restrict yourself to essay questions. You can also organize the activity around reports, evaluations, case studies, etc.
4 You can mix model texts from different sources with student sample texts for students to compare and differentiate between them.
5 Once students have examined the different types of reading material, give them the list of the purposes of each text.
6 Ask students to work out how to change each statement of purpose to make it fit the text, or how to change the text to fit the purpose, or both.
7 Remove the sample and model texts. Write on the board some topics related in some way to the texts. Ask students to brainstorm ideas about these topics. In this way, students can possibly recycle ideas that they have come across.
8 Now give students their assignment question. Encourage them to ask themselves the questions in the box on page 26.
9 Ask students to plan/write the assignment.

Activity 2.3

Constructing questions

Aims:
- to help students understand the structure of essay questions
- to help students understand how ideas are organized

Materials:
- worksheet (see page 39)
- flipchart/computer/interactive whiteboard

Level: Intermediate/B1 to Advanced/C1
Time: 45 minutes

Methodology

1   Ask students to work in groups.
2   Give students the worksheet on page 39 and a time limit to complete the exercise.
3   Ask them to match the eight verbs with the correct meanings.
4   Ask students to use the lists of words i)–vii) and appropriate verbs to make essay questions. If students make more than one essay question for each list of words, ask them to explain the difference.
5   Tell students to write their questions on a large flipchart or on a computer to display on an interactive whiteboard.
6   Go around checking the construction of the questions.
7   Ask one student from each group to present some or all of their questions.
8   Tell students to choose a question to write about.
9   Ask students as a whole class to make a plan of the organization of the essay, which you write on the board.
10 Have students brainstorm a few ideas to insert into the plan.
11 Tell them to write the essay together or individually in class.
12 When students have finished, ask them to check what they have written against the plan.

Activity 2.4

Writing/reading/thinking chains

Aims:
- to help students generate ideas
- to generate ideas in exam situations
- to create an exercise when you, the teacher, have no materials at hand
- to see the relationship between ideas in writing and reading and how ideas can be recycled

Materials:
- pairs of related words, eg, *exercise/health; education/obesity; computer games/ ability; degree/job; clubs/friends*

Level: Intermediate/B1 to Advanced/C1

Time: 20 to 30 minutes

Methodology

1 Give students a short question relating to one of the pairs of words, eg, *What are the best ways to improve people's health?* Write the relevant pair of words on the board or give students a sheet of paper with the words written on them.

2 Point out that the two ideas are linked. You may want to elicit or point out a cause-and-effect relationship.

3 Get students to start making idea chains. Ask them to write down words that are related, eg,

   exercise → health

   health → happiness

   happiness → kindness towards others

4 Ask students to continue in pairs or individually until they have between five and seven steps in their idea chains.

5 You can then ask students to link the ideas with verbs and adjectives, eg,

   exercise is associated with good health

   good health improves happiness

   happiness leads to kindness towards others

6 At the next stage, you can ask students to link the ideas verbally in whatever way they want eg, using *if*: *If people do exercise, then this will improve their health. If their health is better ...* Do not allow them to write at this stage.

7 Ask more advanced students to leave out the repetition in each pair so that they have a chain of ideas: *exercise/health/happiness ...*

8 Ask students to think of other topics where they could use the idea chains to help them plan content, eg, *increasing productivity in the workplace; improving performance among schoolchildren; decreasing the health budget.*

9 Ask students to create an idea chain on one of these topics and then write a paragraph using the chain.

10 Explain to students that this is a useful technique in written or oral exams, when they have to create ideas very quickly. For more on linking ideas together, see Chapter 4.

Worksheet: Activity 2.3

1   Match the words on the left with their appropriate meanings.

discuss   to study something in detail in order to understand or explain it

argue   to convince people about one side of an argument, for or against

classify   to describe the differences between things

analyse   to organize information into groups; each group has features or characteristics in common

evaluate   to summarize briefly and give a general picture without giving details

differentiate to look at something carefully in order to find out about it or see what it is like

outline   to judge the value of something

examine   to present both sides of an argument, to present the arguments for and against

2   Explain in your own words how you think each verb affects the organization of a text.

3   Write out the following essay questions in full:

i)   *outline ways science affect lives past century. Analyse you think most important development.*

ii) *business no place in field education discuss*

iii) *evaluate impact using tax as means persuading people change behaviour*

iv) *differentiate face-to-face learning lecturers independent study/ research. Argue for one mode learning.*

v)   *examine importance university education modern business environment*

vi) *design chart classify body language/behaviour (positive/negative) of businesspeople that could affect business about to set up in your part of world. Write description the classification in chart.*

vii) *technology plays important role all academic subjects its influence grow exponentially. Outline place technology chosen field argue for or against its growing importance.*

Answers

1

discuss	to present both sides of an argument, to present the arguments for and against
argue	to convince people about one side of an argument, for or against
classify	to organize information into groups; each group has features or characteristics in common
analyse	to study something in detail in order to understand or explain it
evaluate	to judge the value of something
differentiate	to describe the differences between things
outline	to summarize briefly and give a general picture without giving details
examine	to look at something carefully in order to find out about it or see what it is like

2 Student's own answers

3 (suggested answers)

i) Outline the ways science has affected our lives in the past century. Analyse what you think is the most important development.

ii) Business has no place in the field of education. Discuss.

iii) Evaluate the impact of using tax as a means of persuading people to change their behaviour.

iv) Differentiate between face-to-face learning with lecturers and independent study or research. Argue for one mode of learning.

v) Examine the importance of a university education in the modern business environment.

vi) Design a chart to classify the body language/behaviour (positive and negative) of businesspeople that could affect a business about to set up in your part of the world. Write a description of the classification in the chart.

vii) Technology plays an important role in all academic subjects and its influence is growing exponentially. Outline the place of technology in your chosen field and argue for or against its growing importance.

3 Types of academic assignment

Assignments come in all shapes and sizes. Commonly occurring assignment types include essays, reports, journals, text evaluation or analysis and rationales. Students may have difficulties working out what is required in an assignment, and each of the above types presents specific problems for the non-native speaker. This chapter introduces a range of frequently used assignment types, looks at the overall requirements of each and suggests ways in which you can help students to develop awareness of how to approach each one.

Discussion essay

Within the humanities and the social sciences, the discussion essay is still widely used. It presupposes that the student has access to a range of sources and is linguistically proficient enough to draw on these to support an argument or discuss an issue, expressing ideas in his/her own words. A good essay thus demonstrates not only knowledge of the subject but also the ability to present an argument and express ideas logically. It is, in many ways, the most difficult type of assignment for all students – including native speakers – but it presents particular problems for non-native speakers in terms of understanding task requirements, language control, selection and organization of relevant information from sources, and cultural norms of written expression.

How you go about developing skills in these areas partly depends on the teaching situation. With an individual student, or a group who are all following the same course, your approach can include subject-specific contexts, as in the following examples targeted at business students. You can begin in class by eliciting responses to questions similar to the ones below.

What is the effect of advertising? Why is it important?

Which advertising media are most appropriate for different types of product? (eg, cars, insurance, washing powder, educational courses)

Should advertising be subject to controls? What kind of controls? If not, why not?

Having found an appropriate topic, look at types of discussion essay question. Some common types are listed below, with examples:

- the advantages and disadvantages discussion:

What are the advantages and disadvantages of being your own boss, as opposed to working for a large organization?

- the for and against discussion, usually on a fairly contentious issue:

Should smoking be banned in all public places?

- the problems and possible solutions discussion:

Discuss problems related to the disposal of rubbish, and offer possible solutions.

- the cause and effect discussion:

Explain the causes and effects of desertification.

Each of these question types brings its own specific requirements in terms of organization, grammatical forms and sub-technical language. Some of these requirements are also relevant to reports, analysis of text and other types of assignment.

Multi-disciplinary groups

However, you may have a cross-section of specialisms in your EAP class, making it difficult to find topics that all students can discuss in an informed way. Once you know your group this becomes easier, and there are some topics that students from a wide range of backgrounds can usually engage with. Look at the list below. Can you add to these?

- *city life and urbanization*
- *education: trends, priorities, responsibilities of schools/government/parents*
- *human rights, conflict*
- *international business, trade, development*
- *the media, technology, computers, the Internet in our daily lives, advertising, news, recent international events*
- *personal health issues: obesity, smoking, stress*
- *societal issues: parenting, healthcare, funding of infrastructure*
- *travel, tourism, leisure activities, sport*
- *work: recent changes in patterns, work and stress, work and leisure*

For example, the topic of urban life can be used as a context for a range of discussion question types. But even question types on the same topic vary in difficulty. Some are more difficult in terms of organization or require more background knowledge. Think about the students you teach. Which of these questions would be difficult for them?

i) Many cities in the world face serious traffic congestion on a daily basis. What are the consequences of this congestion, both social and economic, and what practical steps can city authorities and ordinary citizens take to improve the situation?

ii) What are the advantages and disadvantages of living in a large city, as opposed to a small town or village?

iii) In many countries, cities are growing at an ever-increasing rate. Some cities have more than 20 million inhabitants. What are the causes of this growth and what is likely to happen if cities continue to expand in this way?

iv) Crime is the biggest problem facing large cities today. Discuss.

v) Air pollution is a major problem in many large cities. What are the causes of air pollution and what are the effects on the inhabitants' daily lives?

In many ways the most difficult ones are the shortest, which give least indication of the topic under discussion. Both ii) and iv) give little guidance, and could be interpreted in various ways, bringing in a wide range of information. So, more focused questions are often easier.

Oral preparation is important here, helping to build confidence, establish relevant ideas and supporting information, elicit vocabulary and work on grammar as necessary. Activity 3.1 is an example preparation task for question i) on urban congestion.

Text analysis

Students are frequently asked to read and comment on texts. This type of assignment features in education, social science, journalism and psychology courses, and is also common in access and foundation courses where the emphasis may be as much on the development of critical reading skills as on engagement with the subject of the text.

Text analysis has some features in common with the discussion essay. The student may be asked to add his/her own views on the text, or balance differing views if there is more than one text. However, the ability to analyse and comment critically on information given is central here, and often the student is not required to give his/her own opinion or include his/her own information or ideas. Three different types of analysis can be distinguished.

Analysis of writer's purpose

Students are often asked to analyse the writer's purpose and attitude to the information presented, and to identify the intended audience. The questions below form a general framework, enabling students to approach a range of texts. Not all questions will be suitable for all texts.

- *What is the writer's overall purpose here, and what is his/her attitude to the information presented? How do you know?*
- *How successful is the writer in conveying his/her ideas?*
- *What is the genre? What is the probable source? (if unknown)*
- *Who is the intended audience?*
- *Identify the main points made. What evidence is given to support these?*
- *What is the writer's attitude towards the information presented in paragraph X?*
- *Is there anything the writer feels strongly about?*
- *Is there anything the writer says other people feel strongly about?*
- *Does the writer challenge the views of others?*
- *What conclusions does the writer reach?*

Comparison of two or more items on related topics

Students are often expected to comment on and account for similarities and differences in two (or more) situations, places, objects, processes, activities, events, outcomes, etc, and draw general conclusions. This may include comment on differences between the writers' attitudes to the information, the intended audience, differing viewpoints or purpose in writing.

To prepare students you can ask them to compare two newspaper reports, reviews or articles from the Internet about the same event. Extracts from guidebooks, travel magazines, education, social science, business or economics journals are also good sources. It is usually better to bring in something topical that students may already have some knowledge of. Encourage them to compare some of the following aspects of the texts:

- factual discrepancies (if any);
- different intended readers and purpose;
- differences in viewpoint or attitude to information;
- differences in ascribed causes or effects;
- different levels or types of supporting detail;
- different sources of information or quotes;
- different conclusions, recommendations or solutions;
- differences in language usage: technical terms, formality.

These text features may be difficult to identify. Activity 3.2 gives initial practice in text analysis.

Comparison of a single text in relation to subject knowledge

The text may describe, or be an example of, practice in a real situation. The student is asked to comment on the practice and compare it with relevant principles or theories in his/her subject specialism. This also requires an understanding of and an ability to use the language of comparison. (For detailed work on comparison, see Chapter 4.)

Analysis of recent change

This type of assignment occurs frequently in degree programmes with a professional or vocational element. Broadly speaking, the student is asked to outline what the situation was in the past, how things have changed and what brought about these changes. A detailed account of the current situation may then lead to a discussion of possible future developments or an analysis of anomalies with recommendations for future development. An element of comparison is implied in this type of assignment, but there is greater focus on cause and effect and the language of change. The ability to use time phrases and a range of tenses is also important. See Chapter 4 for activities on these.

To illustrate the steps involved in writing this kind of analysis, you could ask students to analyse data on a particular aspect of human rights in the 1990s and compare this with the current situation. You can then ask them to comment on any changes in human rights legislation that have come into force in the intervening period, and discuss their possible effects. Ask students to comment on the following, citing sources where appropriate:

- the historical reasons for the situation that prevailed in the 1990s;
- examples of the situation then prevailing in particular countries or areas where human rights were an issue;
- subsequent legislation, and how it related to the two points above. How it was drafted, what its purpose was and how it was passed;
- the practical effect of the legislation in similar human rights contexts since it was passed;
- the overall effectiveness of the legislation and possible future moves to amend or develop it.

On business studies courses, students may be asked to account for changes in market trends over a specific period. Change is particularly significant in areas such as computer technology, media studies and design; and students' own knowledge and experience may be exploited here. Changes in consumer demand, such as the growth of the market in organic food in Europe, the UK or the USA, or the trend away from package holidays, or the growth in renewable energy sources, can also be tackled. Provide some source material yourself, but these activities also lend themselves to Internet research. See Activity 3.3 for a task on the topic of organic food.

Report

If a student on a higher education course asked you: 'What's the difference between an essay and a report?', what would you say? What characteristics mark out a report as different from an essay? Why not find out what your students think? Perhaps give them the list of characteristics below.

Report or essay?

1 A set of recommendations for future action.

2 Initial background information on the present situation.

3 Discussion of the views of various experts in the field.

4 Examples supporting a general statement.

5 Careful paragraphing but few, if any, sub-headings.

6 A comparison of two opposing opinions.

7 An introduction focusing on the scope or aims of the task undertaken.

8 Sub-headings, bullet points or numbered sections.

9 Analysis of some statistical information.

10 An evaluation of present practices.

11 A description of the method used.

12 An evaluation of a book, article or website.

13 An attempt to balance arguments.

14 A conclusion or summing up.

Answers: Essay: 3, 5, 6, 12, 13 Report: 1, 8, 9, 10, 11 Both: 2, 4, 7, 14

We will look at four frequently occurring types of report: the report on research undertaken, on practical experience undertaken, on an observation or a series of observations and finally one based on the analysis of data.

Report on research undertaken

In scientific research or in the case of an experiment, a report often uses the following format:

- aims – what the research is trying to find out or prove;
- reference to theory – accepted theoretical framework, or theory to be tested;
- materials/equipment used – listed, with an explanation for its use if necessary;
- methods – detailed description of methods used, normally in chronological order;
- findings, results, evaluation – how far the research/experiment achieved its aims. Did it support/disprove the theory?

We cannot replicate the conditions of a scientific experiment in the language classroom, but a simple survey on mobile phones will enable students to develop a basic report framework in an everyday context (see Activity 3.4).

Report on practical experience undertaken

On higher education courses where there is an element of work experience or secondment, students are often asked to write a report and/or journal about the experience. Where a regular reflective and evaluative journal is kept, a report may be appended as an overview of what has been learnt from the experience.

In these kinds of reports the following stages may be identified:

- description of setting (location, employer, type of business/organization, client body);
- statement of aims and objectives of the placement/work experience/lesson and the responsibilities involved;
- outline of theoretical issues or underlying principles;
- outline of anticipated problems/difficulties and proposed solutions;
- description and evaluation of work undertaken, techniques, materials, equipment used and client response;
- reflection on professional and personal development made (or not made);
- establishment of priorities for future development in terms of strengths and weaknesses;
- summary of practical steps to be taken in light of the priorities above.

Reflection is not as it looks. Students often fall back on generalizations and fail to support general statements with examples or evidence. Evaluation of work undertaken is often problematic. Students know how to describe, but evaluation requires a level of self-awareness that some students, including native speakers, lack. In the activities section are examples of evaluation and reflection based around work experience or practical training. Each one has shortcomings. Let your class discuss them and decide what is wrong and how each statement could be made more reflective (see Activity 3.5).

Report on an observation or a series of observations

Again, this is usually a report based on observation in the field over a period of time as part of a vocational degree or qualification. The student is usually attached to an employer or service provider, which liaises with the higher education establishment. The student is able to observe facilities, delivery of goods or services, working practices, management structures and (perhaps) financial arrangements. He/She has access to staff, management and clients and interviews with these people may form the basis of the report.

Ask students to think about a work placement in supermarket management. In groups, ask them to decide who would be interviewed, which aspects of the service might be reported on, what problems might be identified and any possible solutions. Collate elicited information on the board. Discuss organization and possible headings. A written report could be set as a homework task.

Report based on the analysis of data

Analysis of data is common in scientific disciplines, but also in engineering, business studies and accounting. The student is asked to demonstrate understanding of data presented in non-linguistic form, such as a table, a graph or a diagram. Within this, he/she is expected to identify primary and secondary information, and make a logical presentation. Furthermore, the student may be called on to account for significant aspects of the data, to evaluate, sequence, extrapolate or predict. Analysis is precise and concise, and information dense. Many students have difficulty coping with these requirements – not only non-native speakers. Examples of data analysis can be found in Chapters 4 and 6.

Rationale

A rationale is a document that presents, justifies and, in some cases, evaluates, decisions made or a course of action taken. For example, a student could be asked to write a rationale explaining how he/she developed a programme of events. Guidance on what information to include is usually given, and the rubric is often fairly prescriptive.

The subject tutor may be expected to train the student in the subject requirements of, for example, health and safety instructions. As EAP tutor, you will be concerned with intelligibility and accuracy, but will also need to take into account the need to be concise, precise and selective in the presentation of information, as rationales are usually subject to strict word limits. A typical range of headings follows:

- Context. The student is expected to give background information relating to time, location, relevant people or organizations involved, possible clients or end-users and any physical constraints;
- Aims. An outline of the aims of the project/activity/task that is to be undertaken, what the desired outcomes will be, and how these aims relate to the overall aims of the context organization;
- Theoretical underpinning. The student is expected to demonstrate an understanding of relevant theoretical issues and state how the material/activity chosen will realize the theory;

- Rationale. The student will describe why he/she has created or selected this material/activity, what makes it suitable for this particular context and these aims, what the anticipated difficulties or constraints are (if any), and the means of delivery or presentation. Sources also need to be acknowledged;
- Evaluation. If evaluation is required it is submitted after the event or activity. Reasons for success or otherwise should be analysed, with supporting examples. Recommendations for adaptation or further development may also be given.

The overall text structure also presents problems, as can be seen from the list below. You can give this list to students and ask them to self-evaluate. Which of these is sometimes a problem in their own writing?

- *Presentation of information under the wrong heading.*
- *Inclusion of irrelevant information or unnecessary detail or background information.*
- *Tendency to describe material rather than give reasons for creation/selection.*
- *Tendency to describe events rather than evaluate outcomes.*
- *Repetition of information, or paraphrased information, within and across sections.*
- *Tendency to draw unsupported conclusions or make generalizations.*

There are a range of simple text-level activities that will help to develop students' understanding of how a paragraph fits together, and how text is created:

- Reordering the paragraphs of a four- or five-paragraph rationale or evaluation. This helps students to understand aspects of cohesion and logical sequencing of ideas.
- Reordering sentences within a paragraph, so that a general statement comes first, supported by more detailed information.
- Redrafting text by cutting out repetition and irrelevant or superfluous information. If appropriate, a section of an authentic rationale written by a student can be used for analysis.

See Activity 3.6 for a sentence reordering task.

Good practice 3.1

Liaising with the subject tutor

The English-language tutor is often contacted by tutors of other subjects and asked to help non-native speakers with their assignments. Frequently, the student concerned has neither had language training at a pre-sessional course, nor been attending regular language support classes. He/She has coped reasonably well with the listening and speaking requirements of his/her course, and has apparently kept up with the reading requirements. However, when the first written assignment comes in, alarm bells start to ring.

This was the case with Narjis, a student halfway through her first year of a Childcare Studies, Early Years course. Narjis had spent some years in an English-speaking environment, and her spoken English and listening skills were good. However, it was clear from her assignment that there were problems with both reading and writing. The student had already been told that the assignment needed to be substantially rewritten and resubmitted, and she was already involved in the next part of the course. In terms of reading, her problem was that although she clearly understood childcare theory, she could not apply the principles to the practical situation. Her written English was weak in two areas. Firstly, there were frequent and intrusive errors of agreement, and problems with subordinate clauses. Secondly, she had difficulty in distinguishing language for describing from language for evaluating.

At this stage, when a student is well into a full-time course and on work experience, it is difficult to arrange more than one or two hours per week of remedial language support on a tutorial basis. Sometimes it is a question of a hasty patch and mend. Fortunately, Narjis was well able to articulate ideas verbally, and we worked on translating verbal skills into written forms.

But prevention is better than cure. How did this situation arise? After contacting admissions, it became evident that language testing was not carried out when Narjis arrived, and the course tutors did not know about the English-language support classes perhaps because few non-native speakers come onto the Care courses.

Clearly, subject tutors needed to be more aware of language requirements and of English-language support. We now advertise the pre-sessional programme more widely, we liaise more closely with student services and admissions, we are more involved with testing and we now have a questionnaire which we send to all departments for distribution among all course tutors asking them to identify the language needs on their course in terms of required skills. For writing, we ask what types of assignment or journal students have to write, what guidance they receive, whether they can submit assignments online and whether there is a written exam requirement. We also look at reading, listening and speaking skills. Throughout the year we encourage subject tutors to contact us when assignments are set, and suggest to any student they think may be having language problems comes along to classes or language tutorials.

Activity 3.1

Laying the groundwork for discussion essays
Aim: to prepare students for a discussion essay
Materials: questionnaire (see below)
Level: All, from Intermediate/B1 upwards
Time: 10 to 15 minutes (longer with higher levels)

Methodology

1 Students read the following question. Ask them to comment on a large city they know well.
   Many cities in the world face serious traffic congestion on a daily basis. What are the consequences of this congestion, both social and economic, and what practical steps can city authorities and ordinary citizens take to improve the situation?
2 Give students the task below, as a handout, or on an OHP/interactive whiteboard. Ask them to work in pairs and decide which topics they would include and what order they would put them in.
3 Get feedback from the groups, and discuss any differences of opinion before giving the answers.

Answers: 1b, 2a, 3f, 4h, 5d, 6g

Which of the following topics need to be included in the essay, and in what order?

Topics	Order
a) social consequences of congestion	
b) introduction – what do we mean by urban congestion?	*1*
c) causes of congestion	
d) steps an individual can take to improve the situation	
e) comparison of congestion problems in two major cities	
f) economic consequences of congestion	
g) conclusion – summing up the main points	
h) steps the government or local authorities can take to improve the situation	
i) social and economic problems of cities in general	

Activity 3.2

Identifying genre and purpose

Aims:

- to help students identify text genre
- to help students identify the writer's purpose

Materials:

- texts A–E
- task questions
- map of Spain and/or Galicia

Level: Intermediate/B1 to Upper intermediate/B2

Time: 30 to 40 minutes

Methodology

1 As a warm-up, you could begin by showing students a map of the region, to give them a sense of the location and to familiarize them with place names.
2 Ask students to read texts A–E, individually or in pairs. All the texts, from different sources, are about Galicia, a region in north-west Spain.
3 Set Task 1. Check. Set Task 2.
4 For both tasks, allow discussion if students disagree. Ask students where they get their answers from.

Answers:

Task 1: A5, B3, C4, D1, E2

Task 2: Text Aa, Text Bc, Text Cb, Text Db, Text Ec

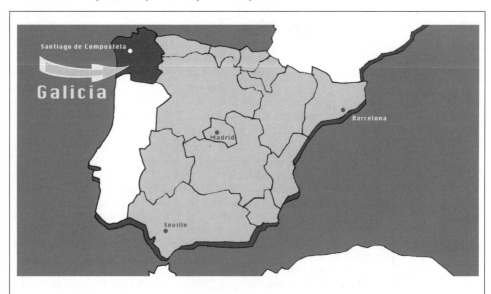

A

The delightful resort of Sanxenxo enjoys one of the sunniest climates in Galicia. With its warm sheltered beaches, picturesque old quarters and comfortable hotels, it is a popular holiday destination with locals and tourists alike. The resort offers a range of affordable accommodation in comfortable modern hotels, but has not lost the charm and atmosphere typical of the fishing villages of the gentle Rías Bajas. You could pay a visit to nearby Cambados, with its fine square – la Plaza de Fefiñanes – where you can browse for souvenirs and local crafts, or relax with a drink in one of the open-air cafés under the elegant 17th century arcades.

B

Rias, like estuaries, were formed at the end of the last Ice Age when, as the ice melted, sea levels rose, flooding river valleys and forming inlets. Rias are flooded valleys in hilly or mountainous areas, and are therefore typically shorter and narrower than estuaries, with steep valley sides frequently rising almost from the water's edge. The word originates from the Rías Altas and Rías Bajas in Galicia in north-west Spain, though the term is often applied to similar features on the Brittany peninsula of western France, and the coasts of south-west Ireland and England.

C

The public meeting was called to discuss the plans for building development along the northern shore of the Ría de Arousa. More than 250 people attended, and a wide range of views were expressed. There were angry protests when a representative of the building company spoke. Many local people spoke against the proposed holiday development east of Ribeira, which they felt would change the character of this part of the ria, still one of the most unspoilt stretches of the Rías Bajas coastline. As one protester put it: 'Look at the coast now. Everywhere you can see villas going up, like a ribbon of development along the shore from end to end. Soon there won't be a stretch of open coastline between here and Cape Finisterre.'

D

One of the major priorities, therefore, is to improve road and air links to the important tourist destinations in the region of Galicia. The extension of the motorway link between La Coruña and Oviedo is now nearing completion. However, the upgrading of roads between Santiago de Compostela and Lugo, and the coastal road west of La Coruña to the Rías Bajas, is still only at the planning stage. Similarly, air traffic to Santiago airport has increased with the introduction of more low-cost flights from various parts of Europe, but an extension to the terminal building to provide a greater range of passenger facilities is now urgently needed. Without an extension, the airport is predicted to reach capacity within four years.

E

The most atmospheric place of all was Muxía on the wild coast of the Rías Altas. High above the restless Atlantic, exposed to the wind, rain and salty sea spray, stands the little church of Nuestra Señora de la Barca. The churchyard, equally tiny, is crammed in amongst the towering rocks, while below the Atlantic rollers crash in constant thunder. The graves and monuments of generations of fishermen lie here, and we were constantly reminded, as we picked our way through the granite slabs, that the sea is the bringer of both life and death. The rich harvest of fish is the economic lifeblood of the community, but the sea takes its toll on human lives. Not for nothing is this called *la Costa de la Muerte*: the Coast of Death.

Task 1: Text genre

Look at the list of genres below. Which is the most likely source of each extract?

1   a government planning report
2   a personal narrative of a visit to Galicia
3   an academic text on geography
4   a local newspaper report
5   a tourist brochure

Task 2: Identifying purpose, audience or attitude

Look at the multiple-choice questions below. For each extract, choose the answer that best represents the purpose or attitude of the writer.

Text A

The writer is trying to:

a   promote the resort to potential tourists.
b   describe the history of the resort.
c   encourage developers to build more hotels.

Text B

The writer is:

a   writing for a specialist in economic geography.
b   comparing Galicia with France and Britain.
c   explaining how rias are formed.

Text C

The report:

a   is very much in favour of the proposed development.
b   is fairly neutral, though not unsympathetic to the protesters' views.
c   agrees that the Rías Bajas are now too built-up.

Text D

The report:

a   is more concerned with improvements to road transport than to air transport.
b   states that infrastructure improvements are needed quickly.
c   is confident that progress is going ahead on much-needed projects.

Text E

The writer is:

a   trying to encourage people to come to Muxía.
b   describing the history of Muxía.
c   describing his/her own feelings about Muxía.

Activity 3.3

Analysis of recent change

Aim: to prepare students to write an analytical text

Materials:

• worksheet (see below)

• websites

Level: Upper intermediate/B2 to Advanced/C1

Time: Varies according to preparation time in class, student research time and time for writing task. Total possibly more than two hours.

Methodology

1 Write the following essay title on the board:
   Account for the growth in popularity of organic foods in the last 15 years.
   Explain that you are going to do some oral preparation for the task, to enable students to engage with the topic, develop vocabulary, discuss relevant information and organize their writing.

2 Oral preparation. Elicit from students what they understand by organic food. Can they give examples? Can they give a definition? Put useful vocabulary on the board.

3 Research (or ask students to research) websites relating to organic food. Ask students to read, comment on and discuss the information in groups of three or four. Encourage them to think about the following using the worksheet below:
   • What the situation was like 15 to 20 years ago;
   • How things have changed and why;
   • What the present situation is, and whether they think it will change in future.

4 Ask groups to report back.

5 Work on organization of ideas for writing: paragraph headings, linking ideas, supporting general statements with examples.

6 Set the written task (possibly for homework).

Worksheet: Activity 3.3

• Which of the following factors are important in the growing popularity of organic food? Can you give examples?

• Which of the factors below are mentioned on the websites you looked at?

• Do you have any personal experience of any of the factors below?

1 Increased public awareness of health issues relating to food.

2 Advertising and marketing trends.

3 Negative publicity about intensively produced food or 'junk' food.

4 Relation to broader environmental issues.

5 Involvement of supermarkets, agricultural producers, government.

Activity 3.4

Report writing

Aim: to enable students to write a simple report based on a class survey
Materials: questionnaire on mobile phone use (see below).
Level: Intermediate/B1
Time: Lesson 1 (setting up): 10 minutes, Lesson 2 (collating data and writing): 40 to 60 minutes

Methodology

1 Give each student a copy of the questionnaire below. Ask them to interview five people each, outside class (not each other).
2 Once students have completed their interviews, ask them to present their data to the class verbally. This can be collated on the board or on an OHP.
3 Refer students to the sub-headings in bullet points on page 46: aims, reference to theory, materials/equipment, methods and results/evaluation. Discuss what information will go under each heading and set the task.

Questionnaire

1 Which of the following do you use your mobile for?

	every day	often	sometimes	rarely/never
Personal calls				
Work- or study-related calls				
Texting				
Taking photos				
Video recording				
Games				
Internet access				
Other (please specify)				

2 Which of these functions do you think you will use more in the future? Are there any you might use less?

3 What developments in mobile phone technology would you most like to see?

Activity 3.5

Statements of reflection

Aim: to develop awareness of what is involved in reflection
Materials: reflective statements (see below)
Level: All
Time: 15 to 20 minutes

Methodology

1 Hand out the six reflective statements below, and put the following question on the board:
   How well do these work as statements of reflection from a trainee on work experience or in a practice situation?
2 Ask students to work in groups of three and discuss the statements.
3 Elicit responses. Suggested answers are given below, but your students may come up with other perceptive comments. This is open-ended.

1 My presentation was really good.

2 The visuals I used didn't work as well as I hoped.

3 My section didn't work well because the person who came before me was useless.

4 My tutor says that I have to use more client-centred activities.

5 I think that if I prepare more carefully things will work better next time.

6 The material I prepared was suitable for the class/audience, but they were very unresponsive. Not a good group at all.

Suggested answers:

1 How does the student know his/her presentation was really good? Does he/she have any evidence to support this?

2 Why not? What was wrong with the visuals? Or did the student use them wrongly?

3 Possibly he/she was useless. But the student needs to say why, how it impacted negatively on his/her performance, and why he/she was not able to improve things.

4 The tutor may be right – but has the student taken this on board, and what is he/she going to do about it?

5 Fair comment – how will the student do it? Where will he/she look?

6 The student should not blame the students/audience. Either the material was not as suitable as he/she thought, or he/she did not present it clearly. Maybe instructions to the group were not clear.

Activity 3.6

Rationale: Sentence-reordering task

Aim: to develop understanding of paragraph structure in the context of a rationale
Materials: boxed task (see below)
Level: Intermediate/B1 upwards
Time: 10 minutes

Methodology

1 The sentences, as printed here, could be given to pairs of students. Alternatively they could be enlarged and printed onto card as a kinesthetic task.
2 Students complete the task and feed back on their chosen order. Allow discussion if there is disagreement before confirming the correct order.

Answers:
Correct order is: d, b, a, c

Reorder the following sentences to create a paragraph outlining aims and objectives.

a The role of catering department staff and students in creating that image is implicit in the design chosen.

b This poster is designed to create an image for the new restaurant and establish it as an exciting alternative catering outlet that is different in ambience and cuisine from existing outlets.

c Finally, text is used to give precise information concerning location, opening times and facilities without detracting from the overall visual appeal of the poster.

d The primary aim is to create a poster which will advertise the opening of the new restaurant facility in the catering department of the college.

Follow-up

This technique can be used with any introductory paragraph of four or five sentences setting out aims and objectives. You can even find two or more introductory paragraphs on different topics and jumble all the sentences. Then ask your students simultaneously to re-create two paragraphs using grammatical, textual and lexical clues to help them.

4 Academic writing genres

In Chapter 3, we looked at text types – the different types of academic assignment that are in regular use in many subject specialisms. In this chapter, we shall look at genres of academic writing, particularly those which are high-frequency and which may be found across a range of assignment types. In some cases, the whole text may consist of one genre, an essay on cause and effect or a comparative text analysis, for example. Frequently, however, different genres are used consecutively within an assignment. For example, a report on work experience will typically contain initial description or narration followed by evaluation. This chapter covers a range of genres and suggests how you might introduce these to students at sentence and at text level, and offers, in the activities, a series of practical tasks to improve students' ability to use the language associated with each genre.

Introductions

Whatever the genre, students first need to think about writing an introduction. What makes a good introduction to an assignment? It is difficult to give overall guidelines on how to word a good introduction but there is general agreement that some or all of the following information should be included:

- Aims and objectives. The writer needs to state clearly what the purpose of the writing is. This may be expressed as a statement of intent;
- Reference to the task set. A paraphrase rather than repetition of the rubric is usually preferred;
- Setting/Background: location and time, event, activity, people involved, present situation or past history (not all of these – that would make the introduction far too long, a common error);
- Sequencing. Outline the proposed order of information, ideas or arguments.

The language used will vary according to the subject, the type of assignment and the genre of writing, but the following phrases are frequently used.

Aims and objectives
Talking about purpose: *The overall aim is to evaluate how far ...*
Other useful phrases: *in order to, is designed to, I hope to, I intend to, it is proposed to*
Reference to the task set
Useful phrases: *The requirements of the task include ..., in response to the above question/task ..., been asked to analyse ...*
Setting/Background
Useful phrases: *takes place in ..., is situated in ..., conducted between ..., look at the present situation in comparison with ...*
Sequencing
Useful phrases: *First of all, before going on to, in conjunction with, in relation to*

Comparison and contrast

In everyday life, we make frequent comparisons: comparing, for example, places, prices, qualities, restaurants, people and jobs. Comparison is used frequently in academic writing too; in analysis of texts and data, in order to compare trends or results, in essays where different viewpoints are compared, and in reports or journals where observed practice may be compared with theory or standard procedures. Some of this comparison is based on factual analysis – comparing statistics or other information on different items for example – and some is based on value judgements informing our opinions, recommendations or evaluation of a particular situation. As comparison is used so widely, it is important for students to become confident and accurate in the use of a range of comparative forms and related cohesive markers.

It is sometimes assumed that students on an EAP course will already be proficient in basic grammatical forms such as comparison of adjectives. In our experience, this is often not the case and some revision is required. Standard grammar practice books will give remedial practice, but students may need additional practice in factual contexts. It is easy from newspapers, magazines or the Internet to access geographical, historical or business data and ask students to compare the following:

- two or three countries (eg, Ivory Coast, Senegal and Ghana; or Malaysia and Thailand);
- two or three cities (eg, Delhi, Mexico City, São Paulo);
- two or three famous places + visuals (eg, Taj Mahal, Great Wall of China, the Pyramids);
- two or three similar events (eg, recent elections, sporting events, conflicts, revolutions, major political upheavals);
- two or three products (eg, cars, mobile phones, hotels).

In addition to using data or visuals you can also use the students' own experience of the world. They could be asked to compare their home town with the town in which they are currently studying, or to describe popularity and participation in a range of sports and leisure activities. This could take the form of a mingling activity.

For an example questionnaire designed to develop use of comparatives see Activity 4.1

Students also need practice in modifying comparatives.

Pair B is slightly more expensive than pair A.
Pair C is considerably/significantly more expensive than pair B.

Comparison is not confined to adjectives. Adverbs can also be compared:

Prices rose more rapidly between 2006 and 2007, fell slightly in 2008, and then more sharply in 2009.

Charts, visuals and diagrams can also be used to engage students in a topic before a writing task is set. Three or four pictures with related content can be downloaded from the Internet or taken from printed sources and used to stimulate a discussion about similarities and differences. Images that work well include three to four different cities, holiday destinations, adverts for cars, famous people or professions. For an example task on the topic of bridges, see Activity 4.2.

Linking ideas

Finally, students need to be able to combine comparative and contrastive ideas within sentences, paragraphs and entire texts. In order to do this, you need to introduce them to a range of linking words and phrases. The following linking devices are used frequently in academic writing. Examples as well as rules have been given.

1 *Despite* and *in spite of* are followed by a noun or a gerund:
Despite *extensive health campaigns, many people continue to eat a high-fat diet.*
In spite of *losing the election the president remained in power.*

2 *Although, though* and *even though* are followed by a subordinate clause + main clause. The main clause can come first:
The president remained in power, **even though** *he lost the election.*
Although *there have been extensive health campaigns, many people continue to eat a high-fat diet.*
Even though/Though *he lost the election, the president remained in power.*

3 *However* and *nevertheless* join contrasting ideas, but <u>not</u> in the same sentence.
We frequently use *however* or *nevertheless* to begin a sentence:
There have been extensive health campaigns. **However,** *many people continue to eat a high-fat diet.*
The president lost the election. **Nevertheless,** *he remained in power.*

4 We use linkers to compare two items to show differences.
In contrast to is used in the same way as *despite/in spite of*:
In contrast to *China's rapid expansion, the West is going through a period of recession.*

While and *whereas* are used in the same way as *although*. They usually come in the middle of the sentence:
The West is going through a period of recession **whereas (while)** *China is expanding rapidly.*
In contrast and *on the other hand* are used in the same way as *however* and *nevertheless* but often come after the contrasting subject noun or noun phrase:
The West is going through a period of recession. China, **in contrast,** *is expanding rapidly.*

5 Similarity. Not all comparisons show differences:
Low-lying areas of London are in danger of flooding. **Similarly,** *a number of other major European cities could be under threat.*

Students could be asked to look at the following contrast pairs and say how they would join them. In some cases there is more than one possibility. Discuss possibilities, and errors, in the class.

1   *sales of national newspapers have fallen/sales of specialist magazines have risen*
2   *there were hurricane warnings/many people did not evacuate the city*
3   *health facilities have improved/hospitals still face severe shortages*
4   *consumption of coffee has remained steady/consumption of tea has changed little*
5   *the birth rate in Italy is very low/in Iran it is very high*

Processes

The term *process* is often used to describe how something is made or manufactured. Typically, EAP coursebooks include a diagrammatic representation of an industrial process, such as glass-making or the production of chocolate. However, there are also natural processes, service delivery processes, research processes – usually referred to as a method – and social processes.

In this genre of writing, grammatical forms such as passives (both present and past) and sequencers predominate. Both of these can present problems for learners, and tutors may want to revise them in general language contexts first, using one of the standard grammar practice publications or websites. But first let us look at some examples of the types of processes mentioned above:

- natural processes: the water cycle, coastal erosion and deposition, animal life cycles;
- manufacturing processes: sugar production, car manufacturing;
- service delivery: the delivery of an advertising campaign, baggage handling at an airport;
- scientific method: the creation and trialling of a new medicine;
- social processes: urbanization, the development of sub-cultures.

Encourage your students to discuss examples of these processes. They could talk about these process types in groups of three or four, and you can give them some or all of the questions below as prompts for discussion, before setting a writing task.

Can you add to the above examples of processes?

Can you describe (however generally) a manufacturing process that takes place in your country?

What steps need to be taken to launch a new product on the market/set up a conference/run an internal audit/set up a new course of study/plan a sporting event?

Which of the following social processes is happening in your country?
urbanization/growth of the women's movement/alienation of youth/increase in alcohol consumption

What experiments, research or testing have you carried out? How did you report your findings?

Do you think human behaviour is influencing natural processes in the world? Can you give examples?

Not all these questions are easy, and you will need to decide which are most appropriate for your students. Where some level of differentiation is required in one class, stronger and weaker groups may be given different questions to discuss before giving feedback. Again, oral preparation helps students identify the stages and sequences in a process, before they come to write.

As you prepare students for a specific writing task on a process, it helps to keep three points clearly in mind. Firstly, what specialist vocabulary and terminology will they need to describe this particular process? Secondly, what language structures will they need? Finally, how can they organize the information in order to present it logically?

Vocabulary

As we saw in Chapters 2 and 3, the use of visuals, brainstorming techniques and questions designed to elicit opinion, information and personal experience from students will help in vocabulary development. See also Chapter 6 for further vocabulary development techniques.

Language structures: The passive voice

The use of the present simple passive is frequent in descriptions of processes, particularly manufacturing or service delivery processes. In descriptions of scientific methods, or of a past process, this may be replaced by the past simple passive. Students from many different language backgrounds often have problems with the passive, both in terms of formation and usage. It is worth working on both before they start to write a process description. See Activity 4.3 for a contextualized activity using passives.

A simple context which generates a range of passive sentences will clarify use for your students. You could get them to make examples about a context created by a sequence of visuals, then ask concept questions.

Example sentences	Concept questions
1 My car was stolen yesterday.	a In which sentence is there a general statement about a situation?
2 The thief was arrested by the police.	b In which sentence is the doer of the action unknown?
3 Eighty thousand cars are stolen in this country every year.	c In which sentence is the focus on what happened to the receiver of the action more important?

Answers:

a3 b1 c2

Alternatively, you can use an inductive approach by presenting students with a short factual text which contains both active and passive verb forms. The present simple passive and past simple passive are the most frequently used. You can then ask students to identify the passive forms, simply by underlining them. Board the responses and elicit the rules for formation. Ask students to analyse the examples and decide which function of the passive is being used in each case. This then provides a springboard for a guided writing task. See Activity 4.4 for an example.

Descriptions of natural processes, such as the water cycle, or the life cycle of an animal or plant species, are often written using the present simple active rather than passive. Processes where human intervention starts a process but natural processes then take over – such as deforestation and desertification – can also be introduced. Secondary school science textbooks or associated websites often contain good examples of these types of process.

Cause and effect

The ability to express the logical relation between cause and effect is highly important in all forms of factual thinking and writing, including academic writing. Within the sciences, for example, the principle of cause and effect is found in evolutionary theory, quantum physics and genetics. In engineering, the effects of hazards such as hurricanes and earthquakes have to be taken into consideration in relation to building projects. In business and finance, the causes and effects of price fluctuations are at the heart of planning. In sociology and education, the complex causal relationship between the urban environment and individual behaviour shapes policy decisions at national and local levels.

Writing about cause and effect can be problematic because English uses a variety of structures to express this relationship. Students need to be familiar with most, if not all, of these in order to understand academic texts and express themselves flexibly.

So, how is cause and effect expressed? The following table gives a breakdown of the most common ways of expressing cause and effect, but it probably will not be sufficient on its own to ensure that students understand how to use the different forms. Further practice is needed, and suggestions for practice are given after the table. See also Activity 4.5 and Activity 4.6 at the end of the chapter. Activity 4.5 focuses on sentence construction, while Activity 4.6 is a text-building activity.

Expressing cause and effect		
Form	**Sentence structure**	**Example sentences**
<u>Verbs</u> to cause, to lead to, to result in Note: to cause is often used in the passive	subject (cause) + active verb + object (effect) subject (effect) + passive verb + by + agent (cause)	a *The heavy snow caused serious traffic problems.* b *The fire was caused by an electrical fault.*
<u>Conjunctions</u> as, because	effect clause + because + cause clause	c *The computer system crashed because staff were not properly trained.*
<u>Prepositional phrases</u> as a result of, because of, due to	effect/result clause + prepositional phrase + cause (noun phrase) prepositional phrase + cause (noun phrase) + effect/result clause	d *The company made large losses because of/due to poor management.* e *Due to recent falls in productivity, the company has decided to close its factory in Hadleigh.*
<u>Adverbs or adverbial phrases</u> consequently, as a result	sentence 1 (cause) + full stop sentence 2 adverbial phrase + comma + effect	f *New government taxes have led to increased costs. As a result, customers are paying 7 per cent more than last year.* g *New safety regulations are not being applied. Consequently, patients are still being put at risk.*

Preliminary discussion of topics will again help to elicit useful vocabulary, reinforce causal expressions and establish patterns of organization of information.

For a more guided approach with lower levels, first set a context using a short text, pictures or a brief video clip – in the examples below we have used air pollution. Elicit relevant vocabulary and put it on the board. Then you can give two model sentences, eg,

Air pollution in cities is mainly due to car exhaust fumes.

Air pollution causes asthma.

Now you can ask students to think about other causes and effects as listed on the following page. Ask them to write five more sentences, which they read back to you. Alternatively, simply put causes of air pollution on the board on the left, effects of air pollution on the right, divide your class into two groups and give them five minutes to come up with as many possibilities as they can. You can prompt with examples:

> aviation emissions   coal-fired domestic heating   damage to buildings
> industrial fumes   asthma   other breathing difficulties

Narrative

Narrative, in both written and spoken forms is one of the most basic genres. Think of novels, folk tales, biographies and short stories. It is not, however, a genre that is particularly common in academic writing and where it does occur, it is often as part of an introduction preceding analysis or evaluation. Even in subjects like history or journalism, the retelling of events is secondary to an analysis of cause and effect or social processes, or comparison with similar events elsewhere.

Nevertheless, students do need to be able to narrate events concisely and accurately, before going on to analyse or evaluate. There is also an element of initial narrative in report writing or writing an evaluation of an observation, practical training session or work experience.

In order to narrate consistently, the writer needs to decide whether the events form a completed sequence of actions entirely in the past, or whether they are part of a sequence that is still ongoing, or has present consequences. This decision then informs the use of tenses and time markers. This seems simple, and learners when presented with verb tense exercises in isolation may have little difficulty in making the right decisions, but often in the course of writing connected text consistency of use is lost. The table of tenses and times on the next page uses the context of oil disasters. You could give students a copy of this table for reference. A technique for developing factual narrative skills in given in Activity 4.7.

Completed (sequence of) actions in the past	Ongoing events or past events with present consequences
Verb forms • past simple (active) *Oil from the Exxon Valdez polluted much of Prince William Sound, Alaska.* • past simple (passive) *Many seabirds were killed.* • past continuous *The ship was carrying more than 40 million litres of crude oil.* • past perfect *The ship had set sail three days earlier.*	**Verb forms** • present perfect (simple or continuous) *The ecology of the region has now returned to normal.* *Campaign groups have been calling for action to prevent a repeat of this disaster.* • present simple *A number of other tankers have serious design faults.* • present continuous *Ecologists are still monitoring the effects on wildlife.*
Time markers • *ago* *The Torrey Canyon disaster took place more than 40 years ago.* • *in/on/at* + past time *The Amoco Cadiz ran aground in 1978.* • *then/the next day/the following day/ the following year/the year after that* *The following day, the clean-up operation began.* • *for* + duration (completed action) *The clean-up operation continued for over six months.* • *yesterday/last night/last week/last month/last year* *It was suggested that record oil price rises last year contributed to the economic recession.*	**Time markers** • *since* *Several more serious oil disasters have occurred since that time.* • *in* + present time *In the 21st century, there have been various attempts to clarify the responsibility for oil-tanker safety.* • *ever/never/just/recently/already/yet* *No compensation has been paid yet.* *New international regulations have recently been proposed.* • *for* + duration (incomplete action) *Monitoring of the effects on wildlife has continued for over 10 years.* • *today/in general/nowadays/at present/at the moment/in the last five years/up till now* *At present, the United States consumes approximately 25 per cent of the world's oil production.*

Description

In academic writing, description has much in common with narrative. Usually it forms part of an introduction to the assignment where the student gives information about background, location, the general situation, or the people or organizations involved. More on these can be found in Chapter 6 in the section on vocabulary and function.

Students can be given practice in writing a short introductory paragraph which gives all the essential background information. In order to orientate the reader, introductions need to be precise and concise, and some students find these two requirements hard to reconcile. Let them discuss which of the following questions they would need to address for a typical assignment in their field of study:

Where and when do the events/actions/research take place?

Who is involved and what are their roles?

What is the prevailing situation? Is there an underlying principle, theory or general background situation?

What is the structure of the organization or object and which parts are significant?

What is the purpose or expected outcome? Are there anticipated difficulties?

Activity 4.4 incorporates an initial description in a task based around process.

Good practice 4.1

Using oral presentations to develop language skills

Some students find it difficult to communicate in written English, although they may be familiar with the concepts and specialist vocabulary of their topic. Often there are problems of organization and sequencing of ideas, as well as handling grammar in complex sentences. These students can often be helped through an oral presentation of an aspect of their topic, which encourages them to use English in a complex and structured way but in an informal, non-threatening and non-assessed environment.

In preparation for a presentation, try to be as flexible as possible in terms of topic. Some students are happy to talk about their own subject specialism, others prefer an aspect of their own culture. Also, let them talk through their ideas informally with you first.

Presentations should be about five minutes long and students can use whatever presentation aids they prefer: PowerPoint™ slides, flip charts, handouts, pictures, audio equipment, etc. Finally, let the more confident students present first.

We encourage students to be comparative, asking them to compare practice in two different environments, or to talk about processes involved in design, evaluation or information gathering. Even if they opt to talk about an aspect of their culture, they can be asked to discuss change to bring in the language of cause and effect. We also encourage students to talk from notes, not to read a complete text aloud. Recording the presentation gives you the opportunity to feed back in detail, but simply noting significant systematic errors or breakdowns in communication also works well.

We have recently used this technique with a range of EAP groups and found that they benefited in the following ways:

- presenters had to be clear in the organization of information and in the use of terminology so that non-specialists could understand;
- presenters gained in confidence, talking at length in an unthreatening environment;
- listeners felt able to ask questions more freely, with less inhibition than in a more formal subject-specific class or seminar setting;
- all students gained in abilities to paraphrase, give examples and reasons;
- students had the opportunity to listen to themselves and frequently became aware of errors they had not noticed before;
- they enjoyed it, and it helped them to bond with students from other courses and cultures.

Activity 4.1

Comparison and contrast

Aim: to practise basic comparative and superlative forms in the context of news media

Materials:

- visuals of news media
- discussion questions below

Level: All, from Intermediate/B1 upwards

Time: 20 minutes

Methodology

1 Introduce four news media: *the Internet, newspapers, radio, TV*, with visuals.

2 Ask students to work in groups of three and discuss the following questions:

Which medium do you use most often as a source of news information?

Which do you use least? Why?

Why is television still the most popular news source for most people?

Which medium do you trust most, and why?

3 Obtain verbal feedback from the groups. Board the tally for the most and least popular medium among the groups.

4 Elicit comments from the class. Feed back on errors in the use of comparatives.

Useful language

comparatives

more detailed than, more trustworthy than, cheaper than, easier to access than

superlatives

the most convenient, the most immediate, the best, the least interesting

other useful adjectives

informative, impartial, honest, up-to-date, shocking, entertaining, reliable, useful

Activity 4.2

Using comparative forms

Aim: to use a range of comparative forms in comparing three suspension bridges
Materials:
- visuals of famous bridges
- a photocopy of the chart for each student (see below)

Target: Intermediate/B1 (also Upper intermediate/B2 with less guidance)
Time: 30 to 40 minutes

Methodology

1 Show students visuals of famous bridges to engage them and pre-teach relevant vocabulary. (Google™ plus an interactive whiteboard work well here.)
2 Give each student a copy of the chart. Elicit oral comparisons of the similarities and differences in bridge construction. Put useful examples on the board.
3 Ask students to determine the best organization of information for a written description. Elicit an introductory sentence and then get students to complete a description in pairs/groups.
4 For lower levels some useful comparative phrases could be given, eg,
   are significantly taller than/is as wide as/is considerably cheaper than/the longest/the oldest/took slightly longer to build.
5 Groups read out their descriptions. Offer feedback.

Three suspension bridges			
Name and location	The Humber Bridge (UK)	The Golden Gate Bridge (USA)	The Akashi-Kaikyō Bridge (Japan)
Construction began	1972	1933	1986
Date opened	1981	1937	1998
Length of central span	1 410 m	1 280 m	1 991 m
Height of towers	155.5 m	227 m	298 m
Traffic carried	4 lanes (traffic) 2 lanes (pedestrians)	6 lanes (traffic) 1 lane (pedestrians)	6 lanes (traffic)
Tolls	£2.70 cars £18.30 heavy lorries	$5 (approximately £2.50)	2 300 yen (approximately £11)

Activity 4.3

Describing processes with the passive

Aim: to practise the use of passive construction, primarily the present simple
Materials: a copy of the text for each student
Level: Upper intermediate/B2 and above
Time: 20 minutes

Methodology

1 Check students know what an audit is. Elicit responses.
2 Deal with any vocabulary from the text you think learners may find difficult.
3 Ask students to complete the task in pairs.

Answers:

1 is conducted 2 are employed 3 are, required 4 is managed 5 are tested 6 is investigated 7 are, expected 8 be given 9 is, examined 10 is detected 11 have, been asked 12 is submitted 13 are made 14 be prepared

An internal audit 1_____ (conduct) by financial advisors who 2_____ (employ) by the company or organization they are auditing. However, the internal auditors remain independent of the management of the company and 3_____ usually_____ (required) to report to the board of directors or an advisory committee. The audit should determine how well the company 4_____ (manage), financially and operationally. Financial systems 5_____ (test) and the efficiency of all aspects of the operation 6_____ (investigate) thoroughly. The auditors 7_____ also _____ (expect) to report on compliance with legal regulations. In order to do this, the auditors must 8_____ (give) free access to all relevant documentation. Accuracy of record-keeping 9_____ also closely _____ (examine). If any suspicion of fraud 10_____ (detect), the auditors will certainly report on this. In recent years, auditors 11_____ also_____ (ask) to complete an environmental audit, in order to ensure that the company complies with local and national environmental legislation. When the audit is complete, a report 12_____ (submit), and recommendations 13_____ (make). In this way, the company should 14_____ (prepare) for the annual external audit.

Activity 4.4

Process and description

Aims:
- to enable students to identify active and passive forms in a text
- to prepare students to write a similar text

Materials: a copy of Text 1 and Text 2 for each student (see below)

Level: All (some pre-reading work on vocabulary may be needed at lower levels)

Time: 50 to 60 minutes in class; or 30 minutes class preparation + homework

Methodology

1 Ask students to read the text about Shanghai Pudong International Airport and to underline the passive verb forms. Ask students to identify which tenses are used.

2 Students read notes on Hong Kong International Airport and use them to construct a similar description (in pairs in class, on computer, or for homework).

Text 1: **Shanghai Pudong International Airport**

Shanghai Pudong International Airport is located about 30 km from the centre of Shanghai in the Pudong area of the city, close to the sea. The site occupies a total area of more than 40 km^2 and is linked to the city centre by major road and rail routes.

Before Pudong Airport was built, the main airport for Shanghai was Hongqiao Airport. Expansion at Hongqiao was not possible as the airport was surrounded with housing. A new airport was first proposed in the early 1990s and development was largely funded by a grant of more than 40 billion yen from Japan. Building work proceeded rapidly and the new international airport was opened in 1999. Hongqiao continued to be used mainly for domestic flights.

By 2003, air traffic had grown enormously, particularly cargo flights, as materials were flown in to keep pace with China's rapid economic expansion. Passenger numbers were also growing and by 2004 the airport was handling approximately 500 flights a day. A decision was made to build a second runway, which was opened in March 2005, and a third runway is now under construction. A second terminal was opened early in 2008.

Pudong is now the sixth busiest airport in the world in terms of cargo traffic, and one of the busiest in Asia for passenger traffic. If air traffic continues to grow at more than 10 per cent a year the airport is predicted to overtake Narita International Airport in Japan as the busiest airport in Asia within the next few years. Total capacity is expected to reach more than 60 million passengers per year.

Text 2: Hong Kong International Airport

Location: island, reclaimed from two former islands (Chek Lap Kok and Lam Chau). Area: 12.48 sq km. Transport links: coach, high-speed train to city centre (24 mins), high-speed ferries.

Previous airport: Kai Tak. Close to city centre. Expansion limited. Surrounded by domestic and commercial buildings.

Development: Begun 1990. Opened 6 July 1998. Two parallel runways, one terminal.

Expansion. Second terminal 2007. Third busiest in Asia for passenger traffic (2005), busiest in world for international cargo since 1998.

Now about 90 international airlines, more than 700 passenger and cargo flights a day, approximately 160 destinations.

Future plans: third runway possible, very expensive – more land reclamation needed.

Activity 4.5

Cause and effect

Aim: to construct sentences using cause and effect linkers
Materials: worksheet (below)
Level: Intermediate/B1 (can be used with higher levels)
Time: 15 to 20 minutes

Methodology

Give students the worksheet and ask them to follow the instructions.

Answers:

1g (has led to/led to) 2d (due to/because of) 3b (is causing) 4e (were caused by)
5a (due to/because of) 6h (Consequently,) 7f (causes/is causing) 8c (because)

Match the sentence beginnings on the left with suitable endings on the right. Use a cause or effect linking phrase from the list below. Sometimes more than one linking phrase may be used. Change the linking verbs to the correct tense.

to cause (1 x passive, 2 x active)   to lead to
due to   because   because of   consequently

1 The rising price of basic foods such as wheat and rice	a) rising sea levels.
2 There are long delays at major international airports	b) serious delays for international airline travellers.
3 The present strike among baggage handlers	c) tests have shown links to hyperactive behaviour in children.
4 Increases in the cost of transportation last autumn	d) increased anti-terrorism security measures.
5 London and other major European cities are in danger of flooding	e) high oil prices.
6 The government has not spent enough money on sea defences.	f) sea levels to rise.
7 Increased melting of glaciers and polar ice caps	g) demonstrations and food riots in several Asian countries.
8 Scientists are concerned about food additives	h) several low-lying areas north of the capital are in danger of flooding.

Activity 4.6

Essay: Cause and effect

Aim: to write an essay on tourist development in developing countries using the language of cause and effect

Materials:

- visuals of tourist developments
- worksheet (see page 75)

Level: All. Intermediate/B1 students may need additional guidance

Time: Preparation steps 1–8: 50 to 60 minutes; writing: 30 to 40 minutes

Methodology

1 Write the following essay title on the board:
   Tourist development is taking place in many developing countries. This inevitably causes changes in the social and economic life of the country. What are the main positive and negative changes, and is the overall effect on society likely to be generally beneficial or not?

2 Bring in some visuals of the type of development mentioned. These could include beach resorts, development around famous historical sites (eg, Machu Picchu), tourists trekking up a mountain, tourists on safari, etc. Elicit responses, opinions and relevant vocabulary.

3 Hand out the worksheet. Ask students for reactions.

4 Remind students of cause and effect phrases and ask them to write an introduction to the essay in pairs.

5 Ask students to read out their introductions. Confirm and correct as necessary.

6 Ask students to construct example sentences for positive and negative effects. Prompt with cause and effect phrases if necessary.

7 Remind students of comparison and contrast markers, eg, *however, on the other hand*. Possibly introduce some addition markers, eg, *moreover, in addition*.

8 Elicit responses to conclusion questions.

9 Set the written task. See also Chapter 3 for guidance on essay writing.

Introduction

Present situation – tourism growing → new destinations

Tourist development in developing countries: examples → change (social, economic)

Introduce essay structure: first discuss positive, then negative, finally give overall view.

Positive effects of tourist development

- brings in investment from other countries
- creates employment: hotels, restaurants, guides → generates income
- income can be used to improve local services: health, education
- creates a market for local produce: fruit, vegetables
- investment in infrastructure: roads, airports → employment
- encourages local crafts, production of souvenirs → generates income

Negative effects of tourist development

- hotels, airports, roads → noise/pollution/litter
- income generated goes to foreign investors → less economic benefit for local people
- much food imported – not grown locally → cost to country's economy
- high water consumption in hotels/swimming pools → shortages for local people, agriculture
- employment is only seasonal
- new problems: crime, drugs, prostitution
- house prices rise, land used for development → increase in homelessness

Conclusion

Changes the local culture → new ideas, attitudes, consumer goods
→ traditional way of life

How can negative effects be minimized?

Are some types of development better than others?

Overall: positive or negative?

Activity 4.7

Factual narrative

Aim: to develop narrative construction skills
Materials: newspaper cuttings, articles from Internet
Level: All, depending on the difficulty of the newspaper articles
Time: 30 minutes

Methodology

1 Bring in newspaper cuttings and/or use Internet sources relating two different recent events (event A and event B). Preferably have more than one source per event.

2 Break the class into two groups, one group to look at event A, the other at event B. Each group should read their information and discuss the events using the following questions for guidance. Group members should make notes.
When and where did this happen and who was involved?
What were the causes?
What was the sequence of events?
What were the results?
Are there any present consequences, future possibilities?
Does the writer give an opinion about these events, and do you agree?

3 Ask students to work in pairs with someone from the other group. They now take it in turn to narrate events in their own words.

4 Monitor for errors and feed back immediately after the activity.

5 Ask students to bring in newspaper cuttings or download Internet articles relating to other recent events for the next lesson. Suggest news items for them to research, if necessary.

6 Redistribute the items and go through the above process again, perhaps in pairs this time.

5 Critical thinking

Critical thinking is a skill crucial to all students studying on academic courses. And while critical thinking is something that students on such courses approach with a degree of trepidation, it is a skill that can be fun to teach and to learn.

But what is critical thinking? In simple terms, critical thinking is the cognitive process involved in evaluating or analysing a statement, a sequence of statements, a paragraph, a whole chapter or a whole book. We also believe that it requires elements that are connected with the emotional side of language learning: critical thinking requires an element of curiosity and doubt. It involves breaking down a text and examining the various parts – almost like taking apart the engine of a car to see how it works. After that, the various parts are put back together again to see if they work together effectively. This then is the process that your students need to learn to use when writing and judging what they are reading.

Critical thinking is really a process that begins the moment your students start writing and reading, the moment they start making choices and decisions about the meanings they attach to what they read and the meanings they try to employ when they are writing. Now we have laid the foundations in Chapters 1–4, we can address this crucial aspect of teaching English for academic purposes.

An alien concept

Student: *You are brainwashing us.*

Student: *This is full of tricks to trap us!*

Analysing a reading text or presenting an analysis of a situation may be skills that are not just unfamiliar, but totally alien to your students (see Good practice 5.1). For some students up until now, critical thinking may have involved little more than giving answers to questions, without any attempt at going through the process of analysing and arriving at some kind of judgement or conclusion. Your students may need to be coaxed into approaching writing and reading in an analytical way, and be reminded again and again in mantra-like fashion that they have to learn to think independently and present ideas in their own way, and not just slavishly repeat ideas they have learnt by rote. While different cultural approaches to evaluating and analysing a situation may impede critical thinking in English, it is possible that the hindrance may be no more than a lack of linguistic competence. It is dangerous to stereotype students from different cultural backgrounds, but it is equally dangerous to assume that there are no differences. This is why it is important to find out what your students want and expect from your teaching. See Chapter 1 for details on student expectations, needs-analysis and cultural background.

Decide how alien it is to your students

If you want to develop your students' skills in critical thinking, you need to start from the very first day. Describing how to use critical thinking requires an understanding of the information in the previous four chapters, as we shall see as we go through this chapter. If we use the example of an argument essay question we can see that from the moment your students look at the question, they are thinking. They are analysing the question and creating ideas.

At the next stage your students, it is hoped, will start to decide what their stance, position or angle is going to be. Some may start connecting their ideas before they take a particular position. As we have said above, it is not safe to assume that your students will have the necessary language or thinking skills to put forward an independent argument, rather than regurgitate someone else's ideas. So you may have to start with teaching a structured way of thinking and build upwards over a period of time.

At a more advanced level this may not be 'honest', as critical thinking requires independence of thought. But for lower levels a bottom-up approach may be the only option.

Methodology and critical thinking

Central to teaching your students to think independently and maturely in association with other students is the methodology you use, the amount of direction you give and the freedom you allow. Too much of either of the latter two ingredients will stifle your students' development. So it is important to be critical and judicious in the organization of your tasks. The first time you organize an activity, however, it might be better just to allow free talking about the topic within a time limit of, say, 10 minutes. You can then build on the task by adding different rules and parameters and varying the materials. You could, for example, encourage your students not to write or even make notes. You can tell them they can do so if they want at the end of the exercise.

It is important to resist the temptation to involve yourself with one or more groups, and to be strict with yourself so that you only make contact with students to encourage them to talk by asking questions. For example, if you were to give students a copy of the list of *Fact or opinion?* statements opposite, you could ask the following questions:

Is swimming an exercise? Is it a good exercise? What about walking? Is one better than the other? Does it depend on the person? Is swimming good for someone who can't walk?

There are many approaches to helping students work on their thinking skills. You may want to weave it through your writing, reading, speaking and listening activities without making any kind of formal separation between the skills and critical thinking. However, we think it helps to point out critical thinking clearly to your students, because it will help them to carry out a task more effectively when they see the purpose of what they are doing.

Recognizing facts and recognizing opinions

Critical thinking can be a separate entity within your lesson, or you may attach it to the four skills as you teach them. If you are teaching it separately or as an introduction to a writing or reading task, you can start with pictures and sentences. You can give your students a series of, say, three or four images along with seven or eight statements. Ask them first to match the statements to the pictures – two or three per picture. The images can be pictures illustrating problems in the world around us (flooding, price rises) or concepts (beauty, age, work), which stimulate reaction. Students can decide whether the statements relating to the pictures are opinions or facts. For example, look at the picture below and the following two statements which relate to it.

The floods are causing considerable damage.

The floods are caused by human carelessness.

At a more advanced stage, your students can be given a list of statements like those below. Ask them to work in groups and decide whether each statement is a fact or opinion. Set a time limit of around 15 minutes and remind students of the finishing time every now and then.

Fact or opinion?

1 Swimming as an exercise is more beneficial than walking.

2 Iron is a metal.

3 It is better to spend money on alleviating poverty than on carrying out space research.

4 The planet is being threatened by the carelessness of the human race.

5 It is more important to improve educational standards at a younger level than at a secondary level.

6 University education is a luxury, not a right.

7 There is a clear link between violent video games and crime.

8 The news in newspapers is impartial.

9 Change is now a part of everyday life.

10 Change for change's sake is wasteful.

Time should be allowed for discussion of the answers. If the discussion looks as though it can continue on its own throughout the class, allow a few extra minutes. However, do not let it run on endlessly as the exercise will then lose its value. An important aspect of this exercise is to show that what may appear to be obviously true for some people is not necessarily the case for others. In some parts of the world – Europe for example – statement 9 above may be true. In other, less industrialized technological areas, it may not.

Long ago, it was dangerous to contradict the idea that the Earth was flat and that the Sun and planets moved around the Earth. And so it is in writing and reading. What each of us thinks is true may only be true according to the limitations of our knowledge and experience. Other people may come along and disagree because they have more or less information and more or less experience. Our task in writing and reading is therefore to convince or be convinced about a piece of information and/or of an argument.

To add variety to the exercise above, you could use:

- a list of quotations from famous people;
- statements that students have written in their assignments;
- statements that your students have read recently;
- news items;
- discoveries/inventions that are contested by different countries, eg, the first hamburger, the first printed book, the first computer, etc.

This latter exercise can lead to a discussion about the perception of events in the world being dependent on where you are in the world, and which perspective you are looking at the world from. For a more advanced exercise of this type, see Activity 5.1.

Using verbal reasoning to examine a text

As an introduction to examining a text, you can start with a factual text or a simple narrative. You can teach your students simple questions to help analyse the detail in a text and hence develop their basic reasoning skills. Look at the untitled text below.

> They hurried away without much attention to where they were going, only conscious of the fact that they had to get back to their vehicle. They looked up at the empty factories and warehouses as they ran along the empty cobbled streets. Some buildings were little more than burnt-out shells, and they were dark and gloomy in the fading light. There was a chill in the air. They finally reached the wasteland at the edge of town where they had parked. It was only as they were climbing into the car that they both realized their trousers were splattered with red spots. But it was too late to change them now.

To help students think about the text, the text can be manipulated in different ways. You can approach the text from the standard factual comprehension angle by asking questions like: *What were they trying to get to? What types of buildings are on the cobbled streets? Were there people on the streets?* Your students can then in groups create short questions to examine the text. You can ask them to write them down or just create them orally.

A slightly different approach is to ask them to look at the text from the perspective of what information they do not know or what they would like to know. This will help clarify what your students read into a text and will help them think more about the reader when they are writing.

Questions you can use to elicit information about the text include:

Do we know who 'they' are?

Where are they going?

Do we know what kind of vehicle it is?

Are they hurrying or are they walking at a leisurely pace?

What are they doing?

How are they moving along?

You can also ask your students to think about what they would like to know about the text. For example:

Who are the people?

How many people are there?

Why are they hurrying?

Are they male or female?

Just from these questions, it is possible to see how much information is not available and how easy it is to gloss over it without really thinking. After you have focused on encouraging your students to think in this way, you can give them another short descriptive text and ask them to generate a selection of questions. You can also ask them to work in groups and add information to the text to explain the context. The best version can be chosen by the class.

Critical thinking and reading

Looking at a reading passage critically so that your students can evaluate and analyse the text requires an understanding of how a text is organized in English (see Chapters 3 and 4 for more on this). But your students also need an armoury of skills and techniques that they can employ to evaluate what they are reading and to judge the arguments, rather than just looking at the words or the meaning. Your students need to learn to form judgements about texts and to test texts against certain criteria or standards. We saw in the previous section how to examine a text using factual questions. If your students are reading a text which contains an argument, a report or an explanation, a similar approach can be used. The class can be divided into groups and given a fairly basic sample or model text containing a reasoned argument.

The students can either be asked to discuss the argument – whether it is good or not, and why – or they can be given a list of questions to evaluate the text. You could even ask them to compile a list of questions themselves. You could use a checklist of questions, such as:

Is there a reason?

Is there an example?

Is there a result?

Is there a cause?

Is there an effect?

Is there a thesis statement?

Is there a conclusion?

You can use a text that contains all the items on the list, one that contains only some of the items or one that has extra items that your students have to identify for themselves. The latter two variations can be introduced after your students are familiar with the first variation. You can ask students to identify any signpost words or phrases in the text like *for example* or *because*, which helped them answer the questions in the list above. Students can then write the signpost words and phrases against the questions. Next, the questions can be numbered in the same order that the items appear in the text. See Activity 5.3 for more practice in this skill.

Evaluating and analysing

Once your students have learnt how to identify the different parts of the paragraph, you can then move on to making judgements about the parts of the text identified. This may be a process your students are not familiar with and it may require some basic spoon-feeding.

Using one of the texts mentioned in the previous section, your students can be asked to judge the quality of the various parts of the text. You could give students a list of adjectives to apply to the text, or a list of questions to examine each part of the text. Some evaluation questions you could use include:

Is the overall argument clear?

Is the purpose of the text evident?

Is the example relevant/pertinent?

Is the reason/Are the reasons given compelling?

Is the conclusion valid?

Is the argument well organized?

Is the language appropriate?

As a variation, you can:

- include texts with a few elements which are fairly good, but which could be improved on;

- use texts where some of the points/elements are badly expressed, the organization is bad and the examples are not good or are missing altogether;
- insert clearly irrelevant statements or almost relevant statements into the text, which need to be changed to fit in;
- give students a list of adjectives and ask them to classify them as positive or negative. Adjectives you could use include *clear, clumsy, cogent, compelling, convincing, debatable, effective, elegant, forceful, important, interesting, irrelevant, logical, persuasive, poor, relevant, strong, weak, well-argued,* etc. Then ask students to use the adjectives to make questions to help with the evaluation. How many adjectives you give will depend on the level of your students. Encourage them to supply their own. You could also make a master list of questions which can be displayed in the classroom for future reference.

By diverting the focus of your students away from grammar and vocabulary, you can focus on the judgement of texts and encourage your students to think about, analyse and react to texts. Speaking practice will help to reinforce and develop the thinking skills your students need, and also helps create spontaneity and flexibility in writing and reading. See Activity 5.2.

Students feeling overwhelmed?

All of us lose the thread of an argument in speaking, in reading, listening or writing from time to time. Therefore it is easy to understand that this is even more likely to be a problem for students who may feel overwhelmed by too much information.

To test our students' capacity to deal with strings of information, a short recall test can be done. This will also illustrate to students what is involved in thinking. Give each student a handout containing 10 to 20 pictures, and tell them they have a few minutes to look at the handout. Then ask them to turn the handout over and to write down as many items as they can remember. Once they have done this they can compare their answers with a partner.

Time should then be allowed for a discussion of the exercise. You could talk about the number of items remembered with ease, the items that were difficult to remember and the thinking techniques involved, such as association or connection. As a follow-up activity either immediately afterwards or in the next lesson, give each student a picture of a scene and repeat the process. Could the students remember more items this time? The process can also be repeated with a text like the one on page 80. In each case, it is important for students to be able to discuss what they experienced and in which situations they remembered more items and why.

As part of their studies, and indeed exams, it is important for students to be able to carry information in their heads for short and long periods of time, and to be able to manipulate and combine or juggle the information. The skill of being able to look at two or more pieces of information in a text or in a comprehension test at a time, while jumping from one source of information to another, is vital. If students start off thinking in English and drop one or more of the pieces of information they are carrying, or convert it into their mother tongue, it will affect their efficiency. Learning to develop the skill of retaining more and more information is about developing short-term recall/memory. See Activity 5.2 for more practice in this skill.

Critical thinking and writing

It makes sense for your students to see some models and to carry out some kind of evaluation and analysis of a particular type of text before they write. The preparation could be done either through speaking and reading, as described in the previous sections of this chapter, or through listening. However, there is nothing to stop you commencing with the evaluation and analysis of a writing topic, then following this with the writing, and then a reading, speaking or listening activity. This will reinforce the flexibility of your students' thinking.

Objectivity and respect are essential in evaluating and describing and also in refuting someone else's opinion. So in writing, defending someone else's opinion/argument or an opinion with which your students do not necessarily agree is a valuable activity. However, it is wise to be sensitive to any strong opinions your students may hold and so at all times flexibility and quick adaptation are crucial. One way round this is to invite your students to choose a topic or topics from a list and to decide on the direction/thesis of the question. But at all times be careful with overtly contentious or emotive subjects. If you are teaching a class where the students come from a wide variety of backgrounds, the sensibilities of each group need to be taken into account. See the sections on needs-analysis and student expectations in Chapter 1. If you are a native speaker teaching in a monolingual class in a non-English-speaking country, or a non-native speaker teaching in an English-speaking country, the same applies.

After the analysis of a task question, particularly an argumentative/expository-type essay question, taking a stance or adopting an opinion is the next step. Taking a stance is effectively like summarizing the whole piece of writing your students are about to do. This can make the first step difficult, even if students are only required to say *I agree* or *I disagree*.

Producing opinions: taking a position

Chinese student: *I thought I always had to agree with what was asked when the question was: How far do you agree?*

If your students are more used to dealing with vocabulary and grammar, ie, using a bottom-up approach, expressing opinions about ideas and concepts and then coming up with supporting evidence will be difficult. We have looked at recognizing fact and opinion in simple exercises, but the next stage we are going to look at is describing one's own opinion. This is a skill which exercises students even up to an advanced level and therefore you can expect to visit it again and again.

As an introduction to expressing opinions, give students a few statements about a subject, as in the fact or opinion statements on page 79. Ask them to say how much of the statement they agree with. You can then show your students how to look at their opinion in different ways. As students are unlikely to visualize this in the same way and are likely to have their own concepts, below are some ways we have used to illustrate how they can think about their position regarding a problem, situation, statement or idea.

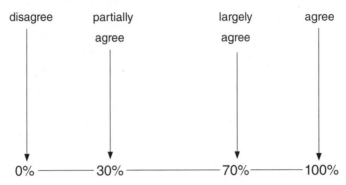

Figure 5.1: Levels of agreement along a line, where 0% = *totally disagree* and 100% = *totally agree*.

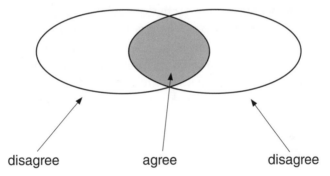

Figure 5.2: Shows the area where two opposing people/discussions may overlap.

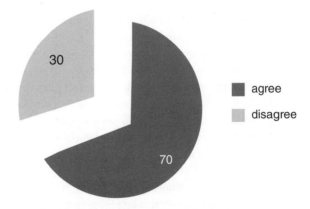

Figure 5.3: Shows the proportion of agreement and disagreement as a percentage of a pie chart.

To help your students develop their position in a logical manner you can use a range of activities. You could:

- get students started by giving them several sentences which they can use to take a stance, or can adapt to suit their personal opinion;
- give them a list of adjectives to help evaluate an idea, eg, ... *is beneficial/crucial/ dangerous/harmful/important.* Then encourage the development of a reasoned argument by using the questions on page 82. The questions can be generated before the writing takes place and can be used as a template to evaluate and analyse the writing once it has been written or redrafted. It is useful to re-evaluate and change the questions at each stage of the redraft, and number each version of the questions. After the final redraft, students can compare not only the drafts but also the development of their thinking through their questions. You can:

i) use any kind of evaluative words, including nouns (*advantages/benefits/dangers*);

ii) focus on a grammar feature that highlights differences, such as comparisons, eg, *this argument/reason is not as strong as/is weaker/stronger than* ... See Chapter 4 for more on comparisons;

iii) as a pre-writing exercise, give your students a list of sentences or a text containing strong assertions. Ask them to take a very clear stance and refute the ideas in the sentences/text using a range of devices, eg, *while/whereas some people ..., it is argued that ..., I think the idea is important/not important;*

iv) give students sentences that express strong opinions and ask them to modulate them using modal verbs, eg, *can, have to, may, must, need* and *should*. Students could also rewrite the sentences using adjectives and nouns, eg, *likely/likelihood, necessary/necessity, possible/possibility* and *probable/probability*.

Good practice 5.1

Beginning to grasp critical thinking from a low base

Siti is a female Indonesian student who is at a non-profit-making language school in Indonesia and who is preparing to go to an Australian university to study law. During her education in Indonesia, she has had little exposure to basic reading skills like skimming and scanning to find her way around a text, which might be expected of students at university in Anglo-Saxon cultures. In the educational system in which she grew up, language learning was based on a strong oral tradition.

As for critical thinking both in reading and writing, she faces a great problem as she prepares for entry into university. Her education up to now has not been based on analysis, as demanded by her university. She has been used to a system where the authority of the teacher/lecturer is accepted, and she has been taught to succeed in exams by repeating what she has been told. Her expectation of studying on an academic course is that critical thinking is not learnt through analysing text independently, but by being supplied with problems and learning the solutions.

At her university, faced with working things out for herself leaves Siti at a serious loss, because she does not know what is expected of her in her reading and writing. Although her vocabulary and grammar are more than adequate for academic study, she does not know where to start. In her academic English class, she has initially been at a disadvantage by not being able to categorize sentences according to function and so not being able to work out whether the logic of an argument is valid.

To the teacher in her academic English class, her questions are irritating and seem to miss the point most of the time, as they tend to focus on discrete pieces of information rather than meaning and function and hence the relationship between sentences in a paragraph. After talking to a colleague who has taught outside Australia, the teacher realizes that he has made assumptions about what his students should know. Siti's teacher is now beginning to teach students about understanding how sentences fit together from the point of view of meaning. Siti is learning how to work out whether basic paragraphs containing examples, causes, effects and simple conclusions are effective or not. She has yet to master more complex paragraphs, but she now has a sufficient grasp of what is expected of her as regards critical thinking, in order to move on to the next stage in her development. Siti feels more confident.

For Siti's teacher, the process has also been a learning experience.

Good practice 5.2

Writing critically

Osman is an Arabic speaker from one of the Gulf States, studying to be a primary school teacher. He is in his early twenties and has had all of his early education in Arabic, with some English – he attended summer schools in England. He does not require a high level of English – perhaps B1/B2 in the common English framework – to be able to teach subjects through the medium of English. He takes a long time to get to the point in his writing in English, but for him, culturally, this is the correct way to put forward an opinion or suggestion, as going straight to the point can be considered rude. His writing goes into too much background and seems impenetrable and repetitive to the native English speaker.

Osman finds it very difficult to express his opinion succinctly and clearly, and then to produce supporting evidence. His tendency is to talk around an issue before coming to the point, writing a long introduction and then a description of the problem with irrelevant background information before he gets to the crux of the matter. His writing contains descriptive details of one piece of information listed after the other. His sentences often repeat the same idea(s) in different ways, and therefore seem very circular.

A simple early solution to Osman's problem has been to make him write short statements giving an opinion or an evaluation of a problem, using appropriate adjectives, (but not too many), and taking each point one at a time. He has been given strict guidelines about connecting devices he can use to steer the way he wants to use the information in his sentences. This requires a lot of practice. He is advised to number the writing exercises he does so that he can look at back the development of his writing.

Osman can now state his opinion and then support it, but when he has gaps in practice, his tendency is to slip back into the conventions he was used to before. He realizes that if he is to develop further, frequent practice, however small, is necessary; and he also now appreciates that brevity can be more effective than lengthy prose.

Activity 5.1

Distinguishing fact and opinion

Aims:

- to help students make distinctions between different types of statements
- to help students begin to think rather than focus just on words
- to increase awareness of meaning in language
- to help students move towards a top-down approach to writing and reading
- to familiarize students with different function sentences
- to help students organize ideas

Materials: list of statements about concepts/list of statements about visuals (see page 79)

Level: All, from Intermediate/B1 upwards (but most suitable for Intermediate/B1)

Time: 30 minutes

Methodology

1 Give students a copy of the list.
2 Ask them to work in pairs or groups.
3 Ask them to decide which are facts and which are opinions.
4 Ask them to comment on the opinions: to say whether they agree or disagree with them.
5 Point out that there is no fixed answer regarding the analysis of the opinions.
6 Discuss the statements as a whole class.
7 Choose one of the opinions and write headings in a column down the left-hand side of the board, eg, *Topic/Opinion, Supporting evidence for, Supporting evidence against, Examples, Reasons, Results, Conclusions,* etc.
8 Allow a discussion, limited by time. Write the students' ideas next to or below the headings on the board, asking the students where to put them.
9 Ask someone to summarize the information on the board.
10 Write four or five adjectives along the top of the board as prompts, eg *strong/ weak, effective/compelling/interesting, not relevant,* etc. Ask for a volunteer to evaluate the arguments put forward, using the adjectives on the board, or adjectives of his/her own.
11 Allow comments from the class.

Activity 5.2

Developing and using recall

Aims:
- to help students develop the ability to think, rather than just relying on memory
- to build confidence
- to develop thinking skills

Materials:
- a short reading text, such as a historical text, which contains basic information
- a list of questions on a separate sheet

Level: Intermediate/B1 to Advanced/C1

Time: 30 minutes

Methodology

1 Give each student a copy of the text.
2 Give them a time limit to look at the text – longer if you are including detail in the questions and shorter if you are only asking general questions.
3 Ask them to cover the text and not look at it again.
4 Give students the questions on a separate sheet. Ask students to work in pairs to answer the questions, without reference to the text. You can of course be flexible about this and allow students periods when they can peek at the text during the discussion of the questions. If you have an OHP or an interactive whiteboard you can control this by revealing the text for short bursts during this phase.
5 Go around encouraging students and giving hints where appropriate. Encourage students to leave questions they cannot answer and move on to those they can. This is an important skill for students to learn, which they can transfer to reading in general and indeed their writing.
6 When students have answered the questions as far as they can, reveal or allow them to look at the text again and check their answers.
7 Ask the class to discuss how much 'recall' is involved in thinking about an idea, etc, and how often they have to look back at a text to remind them of the detail of what they are thinking about. They can discuss how language limits or enhances this.

Activity 5.3

Thinking about and commenting on an essay, text or article

Aims:
- to teach students to think critically and independently about a text and then write critically
- to help students select relevant ideas from texts for their own writing

Materials:
- a text
- both question checklists (see page 82)

Level: Intermediate/B1 to Advanced/C1

Time: 30 to 45 minutes

Methodology

1. Put students into groups and give them a text (any type of text or genre you are focusing on).
2. Match the length of the text to the level of the student: a paragraph of about 100–150 words for lower-level students and a longer, more complex text of up to 800 words for more advanced students.
3. Ask one student to read the text aloud to the groups, or ask students to read the text independently.
4. Give students both the checklists.
5. Ask your students to evaluate and analyse the texts, first using the organizational checklist and then using the critical thinking checklist.
6. Vary the parameters of the task by telling your students that they must agree on each point, or they must agree to differ.
7. Set a time limit as this will help your students to pace what they are doing. Be flexible towards the end of the time limit, stretching the deadline a little if appropriate, but do not overdo it.
8. Check the answers with the class as a whole, allowing each group in turn to analyse a point of the text first, then allowing the other groups to participate. Write the points on the board in diagrammatic form, as described in the worksheet for Activity 5.4 on page 92.
9. Ask students to summarize the sequence of what the class has done.
10. Ask one group to evaluate the text. They can use the third row, items 5–12 of the diagram on page 92. Expect the answers to range from very simple, eg, *the main idea is strong/weak, the supporting ideas are strong/weak* to more advanced, eg, *the overall argument is very logical with very clear supporting ideas. For example, the examples about ... are very relevant to ...*
11. Using the tabular summary, ask students to write a short evaluation of the text using the third row of the table.

Activity 5.4

Drawing a map of an argument for writing and reading

Aims:
- to help students see what has to be evaluated and organized
- to develop organizing, evaluating and analysing skills
- to develop flexibility

Materials:
- two paragraphs from an essay
- the organizational template in the worksheet (see page 92) with the boxes numbered
- cards with the main ideas from the text written on them

Level: Intermediate/B1 to Advanced/C1

Time: 45 to 60 minutes

Methodology

1 Give students one of the two paragraphs as in the materials.
2 Give students a list of the main ideas and supporting ideas, eg, examples from the first paragraph. The ideas should be in a different order from how they appear in the text.
3 Ask students to work in pairs and put the ideas in the list in the same order as they appear in the paragraph.
4 Work as a whole class. Ask a student to insert a card with an idea from the paragraph on it in an appropriate place on the template. Tell them that it is possible that they will not use all the boxes.
5 When you have inserted all the ideas in the relevant place, give students the next paragraph related to the text and ask them to repeat the process.
6 Ask students to draw the template themselves or give them blank copies.
7 When you have checked the answers, ask students to evaluate the development of the text in the same way as in Activity 5.3.
8 For homework or in class, ask students to use the template to write the second or third paragraph of the text, without reference to the original text. They can then use the original text to check their answers.

Worksheet: Activity 5.4

Insert the ideas into boxes 1–4. Then insert the supporting ideas into boxes 5–12. You do not need to use all the boxes.

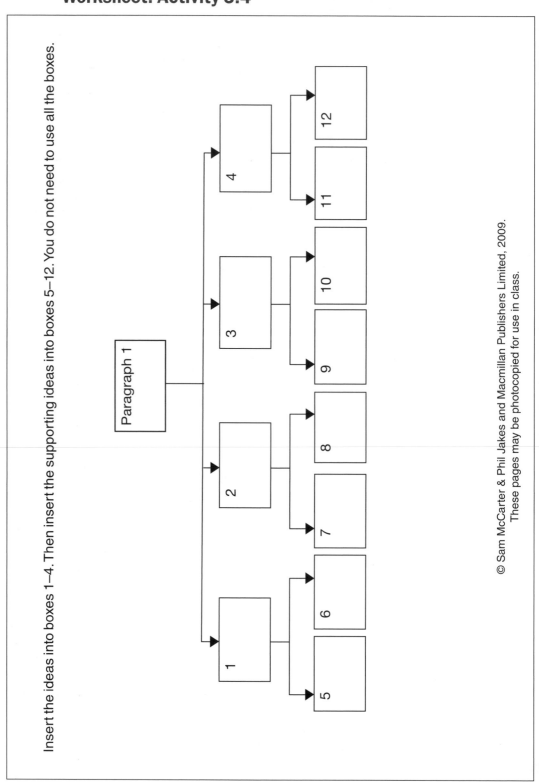

6 Academic vocabulary

There are several different types of vocabulary that need to be learnt in an academic environment. Firstly, there is the technical vocabulary specific to a particular specialism or course of study – engineering, medicine, accounting, etc. Secondly, there is vocabulary connected with study and the educational process, eg, *research, identify, discuss, assignment.* Thirdly, there is vocabulary related to functional and notional categories that cut across a range of disciplines, eg, *location, change* or *trend, aim* or *purpose, measurement.* This is often referred to as sub-technical vocabulary. Finally, there is language related to the broader educational context, which at first sight may not seem to relate to academic study but which impinges on student well-being and progress to a surprising degree. Vocabulary in this group could relate to accommodation, finance, health, rules and regulations.

In this chapter we focus on sub-technical vocabulary relevant to a range of academic disciplines. There are a number of vocabulary books available which practise specific areas of academic vocabulary, but the focus here is much more on enabling you – the teacher – to identify approaches, and on giving you practical examples of vocabulary development techniques.

Subject-specific vocabulary

Subject-specific vocabulary often presents relatively few problems for students already engaged on a university course. However, on foundation courses or pre-sessional courses there can be problems, and it is important to liaise with the subject tutor, who may be able to advise on suitable introductory texts to develop relevant vocabulary.

In contrast, vocabulary related to study and functional/notional categories in an academic context can often cause difficulty for students. Study terms like *comparative, demonstrate, discuss, evaluate, journal* and *summary* may not be difficult to find in the dictionary, but have specific connotations in an English-speaking academic context. Sub-technical vocabulary relating to location, change, time or quantity often presents problems of precise meaning, word formation, collocation and organization of information. But what do we mean by sub-technical items?

The University Word List was compiled by Xue and Nation in 1984. It lists the most common 836 words that occur in academic texts, in addition to the 2000 included in the General Service List (West, 1953). According to the authors, these 836 words account for 8 per cent of the words in academic texts. The University Word List and General Service List combined account for approximately 89 per cent of all words in this genre of text. If students are familiar with the words on these lists, it will give them a better chance of decoding a text. A similar list of 570 words, the Academic Word List, is also available (Coxhead, 2000). These lists help us to identify and sequence the introduction of important vocabulary items, but they are not in themselves very helpful to students – lists rarely are. It is usually more helpful to teach new words in relation to other words, enabling students to make links and establish patterns. Often this is through context, but lexical sets, lexical relations and morphology also have a part to play. We will look at using context first.

Context

Teaching new vocabulary through context, such as a reading text or a listening text, has a number of advantages. Firstly, assuming the context is one that is reasonably familiar to students, the text will contain a range of vocabulary items that students already know. So they have a greater chance of working out the meaning of new items, particularly if they share the same or related academic backgrounds. Also, students will be able to see the new items operating in continuous text and will have a better idea of usage, possible collocations, connotation and grammatical function. This helps them to use the new items to express similar ideas in related contexts in both speaking and writing. Thus, using context can encourage the move from passive knowledge to active use. Reading is generally preferred to listening, as the student is able to go at his/her own pace, spelling is not a problem, and it is much easier to recap if the meaning is not grasped first time round. However, the use of visual clips from the Internet, a recording or a DVD does have a positive role, as the visual immediacy often conveys meaning rapidly. All the same, students usually prefer to note the items down, so put them on the board, or provide a glossary.

If we simply present a text for students to read, without preparing them in any way, they may have difficulty both with the general meaning of the text and with specific information or lexical items. Preparation for reading purposes is dealt with in Chapter 7, but preparation for vocabulary development is also essential. Here are some ways to establish context before reading.

Eliciting context

Example: Eliciting context from students using the theme of advertising. We can prompt using headlines, visuals or a questionnaire, as below.

New advertising regulations for low-cost airlines

You ask: *What do you think the article will be about?*

You ask:

How effective is advertising of this type?
What's your reaction when you see products advertised in this way?
What are the advantages and disadvantages of advertising in this way?

Think about advertising the following products or services.
Which advertising method(s) do you think would be most effective?

billboard   flyers   the Internet   local radio   mail-shot   national newspaper
specialist magazine   television

a new, small, city car   a newly opened restaurant

a new chocolate bar   a chain of tourist hotels

safety equipment for engineers   a university course

Students can answer the questionnaire in groups or as a whole-class activity.

See Activity 6.1 for a questionnaire based around visuals designed to elicit vocabulary relating to education and training in preparation for reading.

What are the advantages of eliciting context in this way? Firstly, students are motivated by well-presented and interesting visuals which enable them to draw on their own experiences and present their own views. Secondly, it enables you to pool the vocabulary knowledge of the whole group, making all individually known items available to everyone. Finally, it allows you to introduce new items which relate to those already elicited.

What are the limitations? One problem is that students from different cultures may have very different experiences and attitudes, and may not relate to the context you are trying to establish. Also, unless your context is both obvious and reasonably restricted, you will not only elicit vocabulary items relating to the reading, listening or writing tasks you are about to introduce, but a whole range of other items as well. Overload is a danger here.

Context from text

There is a close relationship between developing reading skills and increasing vocabulary at all stages of language learning. By the time students are ready to read academic texts, we take it for granted that they have developed comprehension skills at word, sentence and paragraph level, and we expect them to interpret overall meanings and draw conclusions, without necessarily knowing every word. In particular, for individual vocabulary items we assume that they bring a range of decoding skills to the text. These include:

- the ability to guess words from context – both the overall topic context and the immediate sentence or paragraph environment;
- the ability to use a dictionary of some kind;
- an understanding of aspects of morphology and syntax, enabling the learner to work out the form and function of the item;

- a reasonably good grounding in basic English and lexical relations, enabling the learner to decode items through collocation or synonymy, for example.

However, even at this stage there are some students who take little or no responsibility for their own vocabulary development. This inevitably poses problems for the teacher. Highlighting key items and providing a glossary does at least ensure that the student reads on, rather than stopping to question you. However, it does not really encourage learner independence. What can you do in this situation? Firstly, you can simply give out dictionaries, and tell students to look up all unknown items. Secondly, you can set timed jigsaw reading tasks. This is where two or more students read texts containing different but related information. They then have to exchange information, discuss differences and similarities and reach conclusions.

It is not always easy to find suitable texts. Check the copyright guidelines of your teaching establishment before selecting a text to bring in. A range of publications allow you to copy up to 5 per cent of the total for educational use. Academic texts used for reading practice and/or vocabulary development should not contain so many subject-specific items that the non-specialist cannot understand them. This may mean that you have to simplify or adapt your text. Also, you have to enable students to focus on the target vocabulary. The following techniques will help in this: matching exercises, a gap-fill exercise or a vocabulary cloze passage.

See Activity 6.2 for a short demonstration text on travel and tourism, with suggestions for vocabulary exploitation activities.

Lexical sets

In linguistics, the concept of a semantic field, an area of meaning which may be expressed in grammar, syntax or lexical items, is an important element in the study of how language works as a system of communication. Within language teaching, it may be more helpful to think of lexical sets – groups of lexical items that are related in meaning. Focusing on an area of meaning that can be developed as a logical whole enables students to perceive patterns and relate the new items to already familiar areas of knowledge and experience.

However, lexical sets come in all shapes and sizes. A lexical set on a topic like marketing, introducing items like *image, to launch, product, specification, advertising, niche market,* etc., may be relatively easy to put across but will probably only work well with business-orientated students. Lexical sets relating to topics of wider interest such as the environment or health may work better. See Activity 6.3.

Conversely, a lexical set on a broad, non-subject-specific, conceptual area like time presents different problems. Even within European languages time and associated tense is looked at from different perspectives. Other languages have no tenses at all and indicate time through other means. Time prepositions and adverbials also vary enormously. Below are just some of the common time expressions students have to grapple with.

after afterwards at at present at the same time before between … and by during eventually finally for frequently from … to in last later meanwhile never next now on previously recently simultaneously since then subsequently until yet

Where would you start? Well, certain categories can be determined and introduced in relation to each other. Adverbs of frequency might be a good way to start, as many will be familiar from general English. Ask students to place the adverbs on the line below.

never .... always

0% ◄——————————————— 50% ——————————————► 100%

Students should be able to fit in *often, rarely, sometimes* and *usually* without much problem. But what about *frequently, from time to time, infrequently, normally* and *occasionally*?

Similarly, adverbs such as *eventually, finally, immediately, initially, simultaneously* and *subsequently* can be discussed in relation to the sequencing of events.

These are just some of the issues. You may come to the conclusion that approaching all the vocabulary of broad semantic categories like time, location, movement or quantity, is not a viable option. A step-by-step approach is needed. See Activity 6.4 for a task relating to expressions of quantity.

Location is another area of functional meaning that should be broken down into manageable lexical sets. One approach is to ask students to divide a list of items into two lexical sets, ie, *lexical set 1: parts of a country or town; lexical set 2: location in relation to other geographical features*. You could then give students a map or plan and asked them to describe it using the following vocabulary:

adjacent to, area, beyond, bordering, county, district, equidistant from, ghetto, on the periphery of, overlooking, province, quarter, region, surrounded by

You could download a map or photo of each student's hometown or region and ask them to describe it to a partner.

Lexical relations

Another way of looking at vocabulary is to relate individual items to other items in systematic ways. This can be done quite formally, through aspects of lexical relations such as synonymy, antonymy, collocation and register.

Synonyms and antonyms

Language teachers regularly use synonymy and antonymy as a means of conveying meaning in a wide range of contexts. Learners also use synonyms, and to a lesser extent antonyms, as a learning strategy to verify meanings. *Does X mean the same as Y?* is a perennial question. Since this basic urge to relate new items to what is already known is so crucial, why not use it as a teaching tool in the EAP context, either in sub-technical or subject-specific vocabulary. For example, students could be asked to identify human rights synonyms from a list, as follows:

> crack down on demonstration deteriorate disturbance get worse intolerant
> object (v) protest (n) protest (v) repress repressive tendency trend unrest

Similarly, language around positive and negative value judgements, which occur in a range of academic contexts, can be used to uncover useful antonym pairs, such as:

> beneficial/deleterious constant/intermittent extensive/restricted
> improve/deteriorate proven/unsubstantiated systematic/random
> thorough/superficial considerable/slight accelerate/slow gradual/rapid

Individual words could be put on flashcards and pairs of students could be asked to identify the antonyms. The game element adds motivation, and is particularly helpful for kinesthetic learners.

Collocation

Collocation – how words fit together – is as important in academic English as in everyday language. Again, it is helpful to enable students to establish patterns, and to see the language operating in context. Verb + preposition combinations like those listed below are frequent in academic English.

> account for be exposed to compare A with B compare to consist of
> contribute to depend on detract from lead to participate in refer to relate to
> rely on report on respond to

A gap-filling exercise will then give formal practice.

More than 60 per cent of human body mass ... water.

Car exhaust fumes, smoke from domestic heating and factory emissions all ... air pollution in major cities.

Or you could ask students to complete sentences containing the new vocabulary in their own words. This is more productive, as students demonstrate understanding of meaning, and get to express their own ideas:

A successful launch of a new product depends on ...

... can detract from the effectiveness of a PowerPoint™ presentation.

The Human Resources manager presented a report on ...

You could also ask students to work in pairs and discuss a range of personal experiences:

Talk to your partner about the following:

- *a project you have participated in;*
- *how we should respond to increasing fuel prices;*
- *problems high unemployment can lead to.*

There are also a number of collocations with *do, give, make* and *take* in common use in academic English. You could ask your students to decide which verb the following nouns collocate with. Check that they know the meaning of all the expressions used. Sometimes there is more than one possibility – indicated with (2). The study context helps students to remember the items in relation to each other.

an analysis   an assessment of (2)   an assignment   classes (2)   a course
an examination   an example of   an experiment   a lecture   an outline
a presentation (2)   progress   a proposal   reasons for   a seminar   a survey
work experience
do   give   make   take

Again, you could follow this up with a gap-fill exercise, a sentence-completion task or a pairwork task.

Morphology

Morphology is strictly speaking an aspect of grammar, the relationship between word formation through the use of prefixes and suffixes (affixes) and sentence construction. Students often need practice in using affixes to help them understand how meaning and word category change as affixes are added. A very basic format for a word-building task on the topic of study might look like this:

verb	process (noun)	person (noun)	adjective
investigate			investigative
examine			X
	research		X
		collaborator	
	analysis		
	evaluation	X	
assess			X
		X	reflective
		illustrator	

Note that boxes marked *X* cannot be filled. This task could be followed by a gap-filling task, where students are asked to complete sentences with a word that fits the meaning, and is of the correct grammatical category. Similar box charts for completion might focus on academic subjects such as design, government, marketing or engineering. You could also tackle other aspects of sub-technical language, such as the language of change (*decline, deteriorate, fluctuate, increase, trend*), or probability and frequency, where negative prefixes are important (*frequent/infrequent, likely/ unlikely, possible/impossible, probable/improbable, common/uncommon*).

For a complete word-building and gap-filling task on the topic of social studies, see Activity 6.6.

Register

Academic register is usually described as formal. Students who have learnt English formally, through long periods of instruction, may have relatively few problems in the use of formal language. However, those who have picked up the language through immersion in an English-speaking culture, but who have had little classroom experience, may struggle to adapt their everyday spoken language to the academic situation. Sometimes problems of register surface only intermittently, as random errors of vocabulary choice. Yet there are areas of discourse where problems regularly occur, such as expressing opinion or value judgements, hypothesizing, expressing uncertainty, introducing the main thesis or aim, negotiating, and expressing quantity or frequency. One introductory approach is to use a simple matching exercise with formal and informal items, as in the example of opinion or value judgement language below. This becomes even more relevant if some of the examples have come from the students' own writing. In this example, students have to match the phrases that have the same meaning, and then identify whether they are formal or informal.

Smith (2002) says that ...	*In my opinion ...*
Everybody knows that ...	*It is essential to ...*
I think ...	*It is desirable to ...*
You've got to ...	*According to ...*
It's a good idea to ...	*I intend to ...*
I want to ...	*It is generally accepted that ...*

Another alternative is to construct a context in which more appropriate formal language could replace informal language items.

Good practice 6.1

Working collaboratively to improve vocabulary

Students respond in different ways when approaching new vocabulary in a text. Many are good at working out meaning from context, others are happy to refer to dictionaries, but some take little responsibility for their own vocabulary development and are highly dependent on the teacher. With a group of Algerian architects we used several collaborative techniques in class designed to encourage all types of learner to develop vocabulary-building skills. We found that students not only learn individual items from each other, but develop new learning skills as they participate in the tasks.

Using the dictionary

EAP learners at Council of Europe level B1 and above can be handed a dictionary as they embark on a new text, and be told they have to look up any words they do not know. If that seems a little like throwing them in at the deep end, you can introduce supporting activities:

- Dictionary familiarization tasks. We focused on verbs with multiple meanings (sometimes called pro verbs) like *get, put, do* and *have*. This generated quite a lot of enthusiasm, and students were able to see how more precise formal verbs like *obtain, receive, undertake* and *conduct* could replace these very general verbs.
- Text-related tasks. We used a text on converting former industrial buildings to different uses. A prediction task elicited a range of relevant vocabulary, which was put on the board. We also asked students to underline all unknown words as they read, and then to discuss possible meanings in groups. Ideas were then fed back to the class.

Activating vocabulary through speaking

We also wanted to ensure that the new vocabulary items became part of the students' active vocabulary – ready for use – rather than passive vocabulary, recognized in context but then largely forgotten. We used the following techniques:

- Relating the speaking task to the students' own background and experience. We asked the architects to comment on projects they had been involved in, as well as aspects of their own culture such as urban development and change, traditional buildings and climate, public buildings and migration.
- A variety of task types. We used questionnaires, jigsaw reading, visuals downloaded from the Internet and video clips. We also went on field trips to recently completed buildings of architectural interest. These were particularly productive.
- A follow-up writing task. For the architects, we concentrated on tasks that focused on the relationship of architecture to everyday life, so the specialist vocabulary was used in conjunction with the language of location, dimensions, purpose, cause and effect and socio-economic development.

See Activity 6.5 for a task relating to developing skills in identifying sub-technical vocabulary in context.

Activity 6.1

Establishing context: Education and training

Aims:
- to elicit topic-related vocabulary
- to prepare for a reading task

Materials:
- pictures on the theme of education
- a list of elicitation questions

Level: All, from Intermediate/B1 upwards

Time: 10 to 15 minutes

Methodology

1 Display or hand out pictures on the topic of education. Some examples follow, but you could use any pictures that depict a learning environment.
2 Give out the discussion questions. Ask students to discuss in groups of three or four then report back.
3 Focus on relevant vocabulary, putting key items on the board.

What is happening here, and where?
What are the aims of this kind of activity?
What range of subjects and students is this approach suitable for?
What are the benefits and disadvantages of this kind of activity?
Which of these most closely corresponds to the way you are being taught now?
Have you experienced these types of teaching in the past? When? Where?
Could any of the other methods be used in this context?

Activity 6.2

Vocabulary development from text

Aim: to demonstrate a range of methods using text to develop vocabulary

Materials:

- text on tourist development (see page 104)
- suggestions for exploitation of text

Level: Intermediate/B1 to Upper intermediate/B2 for this text

Time: Varies according to the type and length of text, minimum 35 to 40 minutes

Methodology

This text on Courmayeur contains subject-specific vocabulary relating to tourist development and mountain areas. However, the vocabulary from the text listed below, relating to positive and negative evaluation of change, has much wider applicability and we will focus on this:

available, blamed, to blend in, danger, destroyed, devastating effects, fragile, improved, increase in employment, influx, migration, reduce the rate of, serious, standard of living, substantially increased, threatened with extinction, unsightly, to upset growth cycles, visual pollution, to affect, better paid.

1   Even though you are not focusing on the vocabulary of skiing and mountain ecology, it is important to the understanding of the text and needs to be prepared through some kind of pre-reading activity, using visuals or students' own experiences.

2   The evaluative vocabulary can readily be applied to other contexts, not only in the field of travel and tourism, but also in environmental studies, or aspects of sociology. Firstly ask students to categorize the evaluative items using the following grid.

Positive socio-economic effects	Partly positive or neutral socio-economic effects	Negative socio-economic effects	Negative ecological effects

3   A short gap-fill activity at sentence level gives students practice in using the vocabulary in other contexts. Six examples are given here but these could be added to. All the vocabulary in the box below comes from the text. There are two additional items not used in the examples.

> to affect   available   destroyed   reduced the rate   standard of living
> blend in   fragile   devastating effects   influx

a) *Several new high-tech companies have opened this year, which has _____ of unemployment.*

b) *Unfortunately the new office blocks do not _____ with existing buildings in that district of the city.*

c) *The low-lying wetlands form a _____ ecosystem that can easily be _____ by water pollution or unregulated building.*

d) The new college development will make more space _____ for drama, dance and visual arts.

e) Rapid rises in sea level will have _____ on low-lying countries such as Bangladesh.

f) The _____ in many western countries is now threatened by oil price rises.

4 Students could also be referred to websites with information relating to other tourist destinations, asked to summarize the information and report back to the class. You could ask students to look for websites that contain information on the Costa del Sol in Spain, national parks in the UK, the Great Wall of China or World Heritage Sites in a number of different countries.

5 Finally, some of the language could be incorporated into a written task – perhaps on the development of seaside resorts in Spain, Thailand or Turkey, or on socio-economic and environmental factors that need to be taken into consideration in planning new leisure facilities, eg, hotel complexes or golf courses.

Courmayeur

The winter sports resort of Courmayeur is located in the extreme north-west corner of Italy. The town lies at the foot of Mont Blanc. Within Courmayeur there is a weekly market, an ice rink and a swimming pool as well as opportunities for walking and horse riding. There are buses to Chamonix (40 minutes) and Aosta (1 hour).

Benefits and problems of winter sports at Courmayeur

Benefits

There has been an increase in employment, especially among younger people, which has reduced the rate of migration away from the area. The standard of living of local people has risen as most jobs in the tourist industry are better paid than the traditional ones in farming and forestry. Roads, water supplies and sewerage have all been improved. The ice rink and swimming pool are available to local residents.

Problems

Alp Action, a conservation group, launched a campaign in 1991 to alert people to the devastating effects of tourism on mountain habitats. The group claimed: 'Every year, 50 million people visit the Alps, two-thirds of them on winter-skiing holidays, serviced by 40,000 ski runs. This has resulted in widespread deforestation of mountain slopes to make way for new and enlarged ski resorts and ski runs, while the huge increase in winter sports activities has added to the serious erosion of mountain topsoil and a loss of Alpine vegetation. As a result, the danger of floods and avalanches has substantially increased during summer thunderstorms or following snowmelt in spring. Likewise several hundred animal, insect and plant species are threatened with extinction. The several million vehicles which cross the Alps each year are partly blamed for the increase in acid rain which has affected 60 percent of trees in Alpine Europe.'

The report could have added the problems of visual pollution caused by the construction of unsightly buildings, as not all have been built to blend in with the natural environment, and ski-lifts. It could also have pointed out that many of the new jobs are seasonal and have only replaced those in farming and forestry. The change in type of employment, together with the large influx of tourists, has destroyed the community's traditional way of life. The last few winters have been mild, and snowfalls have been light, late in arriving and not lying long at low altitudes. This has increased skiing at higher altitudes where the environment is most fragile. Artificial snow is being used in some places to prolong the winter season, but this can upset growth and hibernation cycles for plants and animals.

Activity 6.3

Lexical sets and the environment: Sorting items into categories

Aim: to develop skills in identifying lexical sets

Materials: vocabulary cards

Level: Upper intermediate/B2 (can be simplified for lower levels)

Time: 10 minutes

Methodology

1   Write each of the vocabulary items below on an individual piece of paper or card. The items in upper case are topic headings. Depending on the size of your class, you may need several sets of cards.

2   Ask students to work in groups of three or four. Tell them to sort all the items under the three topic headings.

> aviation   carbon emissions   CLIMATE CHANGE   conservation
> contaminated groundwater   DISAPPEARING SPECIES   drought   extinct
> fertilizers   fossil fuels   global warming   greenhouse effect   habitat loss
> illegal logging   industrial effluent   irrigation   methane   poaching
> rise in sea level   salination   sewage   threatened species   toxic waste
> WATER POLLUTION

3   Following this, you could give your students the following three headings relating to economic development. Ask them to come up with lists of related vocabulary.
ENERGY PRODUCTION   INFLATION   OIL PRODUCTION

Extension

1   For an activity on the topic of business studies, give students the following headings:
CUSTOMER RELATIONS   HUMAN RESOURCES   MARKETING AND SALES

2   Ask students to research one of the topics using dictionaries, the Internet, ESP coursebooks on business English or subject-specific textbooks. In the next lesson, ask them to report back to the class on the vocabulary they have found.

Activity 6.4

Expressions of quantity: Countable and uncountable nouns

Aim: to develop understanding of the use of quantifiers with countable and uncountable nouns

Materials:

- list of expressions of quantity
- list of nouns in frequent academic use
- sentence-level discrimination task

Level: All, from Intermediate/B1 upwards

Time: 25 to 30 minutes

Methodology

1 Introduce the expressions of quantity below.

> a considerable amount of   a considerable number of   fewer (of)
> less (of)   many (of)   most of   much (of)   one in ten   several
> a significant proportion of   10 per cent of   various   a wide range of

2 Elicit from students which expressions are used with countable nouns and which with uncountable. Ask them if there are any that can be used with both.

3 Put the following vocabulary on the board. Ask students to identify countable and uncountable nouns.

> advice   equipment   employee   expertise   evidence   facility   information
> issue   money   proposal   qualification   research   solution

4 Hand out the example sentences below. Tell students to identify the expression of quantity that <u>cannot</u> be used in each sentence.

a) *In 2007* **a considerable number of/much of/20 per cent of** *the equipment was found to be in poor condition.*

b) **Various/several/a considerable amount of** *solutions have been put forward.*

c) *However,* **only 10 per cent of/much of/fewer of** *the employees have access to relevant training.*

d) **A significant proportion of/a considerable amount of/fewer of** *the money had been invested overseas.*

e) *It appears that* **one in ten/much/a wide range of** *advice was given but not implemented.*

f) *Surprisingly,* **one in ten/less/a significant proportion of** *proposals will not be considered at all.*

g) *We were able to analyse* **many of/much of/less of** *the information from the remaining websites.*

h) *The researchers found* **several of/most of/a significant amount of** *the results were not corroborated by other sources.*

Activity 6.5

Urban planning cloze

Aim: to develop skills in identifying sub-technical vocabulary in context
Materials: text with 14 gapped vocabulary items
Level: Upper intermediate/B2 and above
Time: 20 to 25 minutes

Methodology

1 Ask students some questions as a warm-up, eg, *What do you think an urban planner does? Why is planning important in urban areas? Can you give any examples of good or bad planning from your own country, or a city you know?*

2 Give each student a copy of the cloze passage opposite. Suggest students read the whole text before trying to fill in any of the gaps.

3 Monitor and check answers.

Complete the text below by writing the correct letter in the spaces provided.

Considerations in urban planning

Two major issues face urban planners when any expansion of residential areas is proposed. The first is to assess what (1) _____ the increase in population will have on the infrastructure of the immediate urban area. This not only (2) _____ examination of existing road and public transport networks, but also investigation into the (3) _____ of services such as healthcare, education and retail facilities. All these (4) _____ are closely linked. Pressure on already oversubscribed local schools, for example, may lead to children from the new residential areas having to travel further to school, (5) _____ increasing traffic at peak periods.

(6) _____, while population expansion may lead to an increase in turnover for retail outlets, if there is no provision for local shops within walking distance, then congestion on roads is (7) _____ to increase. If shops are not within walking distance, and there are no buses or other (8) _____ of public transport, all shopping will be done by car. Residents will also have to drive if there is no local doctor's surgery.

The second major issue is social (9) _____ than economic. Who are the people who will come to live in these new dwellings? Where will they work, and what is the social demographic? Will they be (10) _____ young people, living alone or in couples without children, or families with school-age children? Will some of them work in (11) _____ public services such as education, healthcare or the police force, who have recently had particular difficulty getting on the property ladder? If so, a certain (12) _____ of affordable homes may have to be built for these key workers. And how will a sense of social cohesion be (13) _____ amongst a population that comes from different locations and backgrounds, that has different aspirations and has no communal (14) _____ in the immediate neighbourhood through which to meet and make new friends?

1 a) interest	b) result	c) solution	d) impact
2 a) involves	b) consists	c) expects	d) produces
3 a) demand	b) provision	c) protection	d) amount
4 a) subjects	b) factors	c) suggestions	d) outcomes
5 a) although	b) finally	c) thus	d) however
6 a) Similarly	b) Finally	c) Rapidly	d) Subsequently
7 a) probable	b) likely	c) usually	d) proposed
8 a) measures	b) stops	c) sectors	d) forms
9 a) rather	b) fewer	c) enough	d) higher
10 a) preferred	b) predicted	c) presumably	d) predominantly
11 a) effective	b) general	c) essential	d) widespread
12 a) degree	b) quality	c) percentage	d) majority
13 a) produced	b) demanded	c) established	d) presented
14 a) systems	b) facilities	c) designs	d) requirements

Answers:
1d 2a 3b 4b 5c 6a 7b 8d 9a 10d 11c 12c 13c 14b

Activity 6.6

Morphology: Negative prefixes (Context: Social studies)

Aim: to develop understanding of negative prefixes through an identification task
Materials:
- list of prefixes
- boxed adjectives

Level: Upper intermediate/B2 (general academic words could be introduced for lower levels)
Time: 10 to 15 minutes

Methodology

1 Write the negative prefixes *in, im, il, ir, un* and *dis* on the board.
2 Distribute flashcards of the following words and ask students to sort into categories. Monitor, assist and obtain feedback.

> biased   censored   effective   elected   equal   honest
> humane   just   legal   legitimate   patient   permanent
> plausible   proportionate   protected   reconcilable
> responsible   tolerant   trusted

3 Ask students to work in pairs and match the prefixes with the words, to form new words.
4 Ask students to match the same prefixes with vocabulary from wider academic contexts, eg,
    common, connected, corroborated, feasible, logical, organized, practical, regular, relevant, reversible, satisfied, scientific, significant, soluble, systematic, tested.

7 Giving feedback and redrafting

'Only people who do nothing make no mistakes.'

With the length and relative importance of some written work that EAP teachers have to mark and grade, the pressure can be great. In this situation, giving feedback to students through corrected written work can so easily become incidental to the learning process, especially in classes with large numbers or where teachers have a heavy workload. If it is not managed properly, the correction/feedback process can then end up, for teacher and student alike, a waste of time. And even if you are prepared, the emotion that so inevitably surrounds receiving and indeed giving feedback – trepidation or anticipation, disappointment, resignation or indifference – can turn a class or tutorial into a disaster. But this need not be the case. This 'chore' for teachers and students can be turned into something positive. If we think in terms of mistakes, errors and corrections, then our outlook is bound to be negative. However, if you explain to students that mistakes give them the opportunity to test their knowledge of grammar, vocabulary and knowledge against yours, then mistakes can perhaps come to be seen as acts of creation, as attempts at being perfect. This is not to advocate a swing to the extreme where everything is correct and perfect, but to consider a different attitude towards correcting student work.

Correcting your students' written work:

- gives you feedback about what they have learnt and improves your knowledge;
- improves their work;
- gives you feedback about what you have taught;
- shows what your students do not know;
- shows students what they know and do not know;
- helps you to develop your teaching;
- helps steer students in the right direction.

Student mistakes: Just a learning tool?

Your students are on a journey towards mastering the English language. Along the way, their knowledge will evolve and perspectives may change. As the teacher, you can make it a pleasant trip or a bumpy ride.

For you the teacher, dealing with correction and feedback can be a positive experience, with your students being used as a source of learning. When you give back written work to a class, it is useful to ascertain how students react to your feedback, as this can inform your feedback techniques. Over time, you will be able to gauge how much they can take by way of comment. A simple technique to gauge what students think of corrected work they have done is to watch what they do when you give it back: what is their facial expression when they look at the page? (horror, delight, disappointment, anger, frustration or a mixture of these, or indifference); do they look at the bottom of the page for the global mark/comment? The number of mistakes? Do they fold it up or even it screw it up and leave it sitting on the desk when they leave the classroom? Or do they number and date it, if they have not already done so, and put it in a folder in perfect order, to be produced when called upon?

It is so easy to walk around a classroom handing back written work, and not notice students' reactions. We may feel we know what students think, but until we check our assumptions we are missing out on valuable information. This feedback you can obtain from your students' reactions can inform your teaching and help to shape how you handle feedback and ultimately refine your teaching. Correction and feedback are as much a teaching as they are a learning tool. So it is useful if you as a teacher are as aware of the non-verbal reactions of your students as you are of any verbal feedback.

Pre-correction preparation techniques

Before you correct students' written work, decide:

- what to focus on. Are you going to correct all the mistakes regardless? Or will you focus on one particular area? Possible areas include spelling; connectives; subject/verb agreement; singulars and plurals; sentences with no verb or main clause; poor sequence of tenses; sentences where the grammar is inconsistent; word order; systematic, repeated errors; errors that impede or could impede intelligibility; and errors relating to what you have just taught them. Will you ignore random slips, simply underlining them and leaving them for self-correction? Or will you use a mixture of these approaches?
- how much to correct. Are you going to correct every mistake because it is important for students to see them all? Even if they faint when they see the page?
- the pattern of the corrections on the page. Are they all going to be bunched together or perhaps spread around the page? For example, if you choose the mistakes to correct carefully, you can ensure they are spread throughout the text (with perhaps no more than an average of maybe one every two lines). Then the mistakes will look more accessible, rather than being concentrated in one place.
- what system you are going to use. Are you going to correct the mistakes? Will you code them for students to correct? Or will you identify the mistakes somehow and ask students to decide what type of mistake it is, and what the correction is?
- how you would react if someone gave you the text you have just corrected.

Another part of preparing for correction is discussing with students how work should be presented. If you have to correct work that is handwritten or typed, encourage your students to use double spacing and margins, preferably on both sides of the text. If a piece of writing is tightly spaced, it will be difficult to read, even for the student who wrote it.

Correcting a text

You can approach the correction of your students' written work with a bottom-up approach. This means you look through the text at the word and phrase level, then move up to the clause level, then up to the sentence level, then the paragraphs and sections, and finally the whole text. Or you can use a top-down approach, working in the opposite direction by starting with the whole text and moving down to the individual words. At any one time you may want to focus only on one level, but as your students become more advanced, you can start approaching it with a bottom-up and top-down approach simultaneously.

If we start at the word level, it is probably better for you and your students to begin by deciding how much to correct. There is nothing more dispiriting for a student than receiving a piece of paper covered in red ink, regardless of how much they protest and say to you that it is what they want. No, what they really want is a clean sheet with the top mark written on it. This effectively brings us to the crux of the correcting process: the attitude, the personality and the self-awareness of the student; and to a degree the corrector. These dictate how successful your correcting will be and whether students take on board what you say. The success of the correcting process depends on taking into account and addressing these emotions.

It is worth remembering that corrections can be seen as an attack on the individual, the ego, even the culture of the student. So part of the process is teaching students to be able to receive and absorb the corrections, so they will benefit from them. Otherwise, the same mistakes are repeated again and again. Does it sound all too familiar?

When correcting, it is essential to indicate as far as possible the good parts of the text by ticking or highlighting them in some way. This can help to mitigate the correction of mistakes.

Correction at the word level: Bottom-up approach

You can limit your correction and correct a number of words that your students can handle. This obviously depends on the length of the text, but if you judiciously spread the corrections over the page and aim for about one correction every 15 to 20 words, or one correction every two lines in a text of 250 to 300 words, the text returned to the student will not look so daunting.

Whatever the level, the easiest type of correction to focus on is spelling. Time permitting, you can give students alternative spellings on their written work to choose from. When you get to know your students better, you can make the spelling corrections student-specific, based on the kinds of mistake the students normally make. This of course involves extra time, but if you make correction and feedback an integral part of the lesson and use it as a teaching tool, it can save time in the long run, as mistakes become fewer. Alternatively, you can use a code for spelling mistakes, such as *(sp)*. Then, during a lesson, you can give students access to dictionaries and ask them to correct their own or their partner's spelling mistakes.

You could also leave three or four mistakes unmarked, for students to find themselves. To increase flexibility, you can do a mixture of coding, correcting, giving alternatives and leaving some words uncorrected. See Activity 7.1.

You may also want to limit your corrections to a particular area, like punctuation. If there are not enough mistakes in this area, you may want to treat them as incidental mistakes. However, as punctuation is an area that many students find difficult, it may be worth using punctuation as a focus of feedback and as an excuse to do some remedial teaching.

Engaging students in the correcting process

'Use double-spacing even in handwritten work, as it will make it easier for you to see your own mistakes.'

If you are introducing a class to written feedback, you can put a selection of incorrect words/items that they have used in writing on the board, with alternatives, and ask them to choose the correct alternative. You could also then code the errors to show what kind of mistakes they are.

Alternatively, you can put a short model/sample text on the board, or copy it and give it to students as a handout. This model text will contain corrections and will show the marking system you will use now and in future for correcting spelling.

Learning to see mistakes in what we have written is a slow process. When we look at a text, the mind automatically seeks to make sense of it, so that the mistakes fall below the radar. To help your students, you can show them a text on an OHP and ask them to find three or four obvious mistakes, giving them a very short time limit to see the text. Then cover the text again. The exercise can be repeated several times until someone or all of them have found the mistakes. You can do the same thing with paper, telling students to turn the page over and insisting that they follow your verbal instructions exactly. In effect, your students are being taught to scan the text, so you can point out the techniques described in Chapter 2, page 32.

A very simple, but effective, variation of the scanning technique is to encourage your students to scan for mistakes from right to left. There will of course be words like *learn/lean* or *hair/hare* that will slip through, but it is still a useful technique, as students are looking for a word picture rather than scanning for meaning.

Types of mistakes

Mistakes come in all shapes and sizes, and include:

- individual/idiosyncratic errors;
- first-/second-language interference/transfer;
- slips of the pen/typing errors;
- poor dictionary use;
- oversimplification due to the use of electronic dictionaries, which may not take into account multiple meanings;
- homonyms;
- lack of knowledge;
- style;
- register;
- punctuation.

See Activity 7.2.

Language transfer is now viewed positively by some, as not everything that a student translates from their own language into English is wrong. An interest in and even rudimentary knowledge of a smattering of languages can help you understand where your students are coming from as you correct their work. Few of us have the time to learn about all the types of mistakes that may occur as a result of first-/second-language interference. However, it is desirable for all of us to learn as much as possible about the languages of the students we are teaching. A bank of knowledge can be built up by asking your students about discrete items, like vocabulary for different colours or whether they have an equivalent of the present continuous. It is easy to assume that because this tense is found in English that all languages have it. Is it part of the grammar in Arabic, Chinese, French, Japanese, Russian or Urdu? If not, this will help you understand why some students make the mistakes they do, and you can accommodate them in your explanations.

If you want to highlight the differences between languages for your students and build a record for yourself, you could make a table, as below. The table could also be adapted to include positive examples of language transfer.

Language item	Language	Difference
Present simple/Present continuous		
Simple past/Present perfect		
Present perfect continuous/Present continuous		
Inflection in verbs		
Active/Passive		
Articles		
Tenses generally		
Adjectives with s added		
Script		

Larger chunks of text: Top-down approach

At lower levels, you may be more involved with correcting mistakes at the word or phrase level, but as students progress you can gradually introduce corrections related to cohesion and coherence. Where there is a problem with connections between clauses, sentences or paragraphs, you could just write down the required word or phrase and ask the student to think about it, and tell you later how to rewrite the text.

Changes to larger chunks of text require greater knowledge, so for lower levels it is obviously better to restrict your comments to a few points per piece of work. If a piece of writing is full of basic mistakes at a word level, there is little point attempting to correct at a clause/sentence/paragraph level. To help students, encourage them to read (see Chapter 8) and take every opportunity to point out how texts are organized.

If you are with a class long enough, you may find that as your students' awareness of the features of different text types increases, as described in Chapter 4, the volume of mistakes will decrease. Gradually, they will become more focused as certain things become automatic.

Building a learning relationship with students

How can you use your students' mistakes to build a learning relationship? All of us have mistakes that we repeatedly make, so a simple technique to help you engage with your students is to learn a few mistakes that relate to each student. In a large class, you may think that this is daunting because you will not be able to remember all the students' mistakes. However, work smart! Learn as many as you can, maybe two or three idiosyncratic mistakes per student – for example, forgetting to add *s* to third-person singular verbs. Then, when you give feedback next time, or even during an exercise in the class, you refer to the student's previous homework and remind him/her of the mistake. Tying students' mistakes to the whole learning process helps to pre-empt mistakes and helps you and your students to take mistakes seriously.

If you are sharing a class with other teachers, another way of bringing mistakes and feedback into the heart of the lesson is to share the marking.

Let us say you are teaching an intensive class with another teacher, and you teach on Tuesdays. A way of binding the class close together is for you to mark the work set by the teacher on the Monday and then for the teacher who teaches on Wednesday to mark the work set on the Tuesday. You may not of course be giving students written work every day. But on intensive courses, this method works well, as it helps you and your fellow teachers see that you are following a syllabus.

Corrections and giving feedback

Once you start correcting a piece of written work, you are giving feedback. If you are using feedback to build your students' confidence as well as to address the problems that your students face, it is logical that the feedback should be positive, without missing out on the essential aspects of correction. Giving positive feedback first is not just about being nice for the sake of it. It is difficult for all of us to accept criticism, but if the way is prepared then we are all more likely to accept it.

We all want to be perfect and present ourselves in a good light. If someone criticizes us in front of other people, we feel uncomfortable. Students are no different. So be prepared to say something positive before you make a criticism: *This is good. I like this, but where you can improve is ...* Then select several things to focus on. Let's say you made 12 corrections to a piece of writing. Three or four can be selected as the main areas for the student to focus on. The rest can be mentioned as minor, but worth noting. By creating a hierarchy for students' mistakes in this way, you can lessen their impact and increase the effectiveness of your correction process.

The emotional reaction to your feedback may then be reduced. You can advise students that there are only one or two things to watch out for, but they should always check for minor mistakes too. This may leave your students smiling, rather than frowning. You also could encourage your students to keep a formal record of their mistakes.

There is something final about written feedback, which can be tempered as described above. If students are simply handed back their work without any individual feedback from the tutor, you will no doubt notice that their eyes focus on the global mark and then move to the corrections. However, in a one-to-one tutorial, the feedback you give will be more individual/personal rather than being directed at a class in general. It may be more detailed, even more radical. The same basic principles of correction and feedback apply, but perhaps an added awareness of or sensitivity to the individual student is advisable.

Using the student as your guide, you could begin by asking the student what he/she expects. Once you have given your feedback, you can then add a few extra pieces of advice to help the student. You can guide the student, rather than be prescriptive, using questions like:

Is there a better way to rephrase this section?
Could another example be given here, or a more pertinent example?
Would this be better ...?
Do you think this needs to be expanded on/shortened?

Time, organization and feedback

There is no escaping the burden of time that feedback imposes on the teacher. However, there are strategies you can use to lessen this problem. In a student-centred approach, you can overcome this by making the individual feedback verbal and most/ some of the written feedback general. For example, if you are giving written work back in class, do so while your students are engaged in another activity. Always try to say something to every student. You could try to plan the written task in advance so that it fits in with the time you have earmarked for feedback. This method helps to reduce the impact of open criticism in front of the class. The personal touch of talking to a student – even if it is only for a few seconds – is invaluable, and often preferable to infrequent, long meetings. Short, regular debriefs with students can help prevent larger problems brewing up over time.

Feedback and advanced students

With more advanced students, while at the same time highlighting the good parts with underlining and ticking, you might reduce the correction of the work to coding, so that students have to work out the mistake and correction themselves. More advanced students producing longer pieces of written work will probably have invested more time than those at lower levels, especially if they are writing pieces of work that run into hundreds or thousands of words. Again, balancing positive and constructive feedback is essential if you are to help the student develop and keep him/her on board.

In addition to the methods of giving feedback described above, you can make feedback into an active activity. You can put question marks next to items that need improvement, or correct and underline the good points in a text or write *Yes!* next to them. You need to be judicious here and work out a hierarchy of positive statements, because once you have said *excellent*, you have limited yourself and the student.

Personal mistakes and independence

'I haven't made any progress.'

Self-feedback is a way of encouraging students to review their work. It is not easy for any of us, let alone students, to see how we have improved and to learn from our mistakes. As a way of overcoming this, periodically you can ask students to bring in a selection of their work – say the last four or five pieces of writing – and have them work in pairs and explain to each other how their writing has improved. The same can be done in a tutorial, with the student taking the lead and explaining to you his/her development.

Dealing with correction and feedback in this way may seem time-consuming. However, by making feedback learner-centred, the initial investment in time soon pays off. The benefit for students is that they learn from their mistakes, see how far they have come and where they can go. It encourages them to take responsibility for their own mistakes and development. As the teacher, you have a better opportunity to learn about your students and connect with them. All of this can lighten your burden and help your students at the same time.

Another way to encourage students to take responsibility for their mistakes is to ask them to keep a record of their language use – when they get things wrong, and when they get them right. Adding to this record could be a regular classroom activity, every week or fortnight. You could use a template like the one below.

	Date	Date	Date	Date
sp *receive*	✔			✗
subject–verb agreement	✗	✔		
singular/plural	✗	✗	✔	

Once students have identified their mistakes, they can monitor them over time and see where they have made improvements. This will also help focus students on their more stubborn mistakes and, while they might never disappear, at least they may be reduced.

To help your students hone their self-correction techniques, you can encourage them to question everything that they write. You can teach them questions like those on pages 81 and 82, Chapter 5. Or you can put them into groups and ask them to develop a set of questions for examining a word:

Is the spelling correct?

Is it the right word?

Is it the right part of speech?

Is the word repeated from before?

Is it singular/plural?

Doe it fit with other words in the phrase?

A similar set of questions can be drawn up to consider phrases/sentences:

Are the ideas related?

Is the relationship signposted correctly?

Is the clause/sentence relevant or irrelevant?

These questions can be developed and used by the whole class.

Redrafting

Learning to redraft is an important skill for all students to learn. However, it is also important that students do not get addicted to redrafting – they also need to be able to write under exam conditions, when they will not have time to rewrite. So students need to learn both skills.

When giving feedback about redrafting to students of any level, it may be wise to think about doing it in waves. Even with lower-level students, when you are focusing on individual items in the text as described above, redrafting can help. They can be asked to write/type a clean copy in class after you have given back the homework. One way of encouraging your students to start working on feedback and rewriting is to tell them that you are available to answer any questions/doubts that they have before they begin redrafting.

Students will also sense whether you are confident about giving feedback. The more confident you are, the more likely they are to ask you for help and perhaps listen to you.

Correction in waves

When asking your students to redraft a piece of writing, the question of how much to ask the students to correct arises. For example, do you ask students to rewrite simultaneously items that are related to individual words like spelling, and chunks of text? Or do you want these corrections to be done separately? It depends on the student. For lower-level students it may be overwhelming to attempt to do them together, and so it might be better to have them redraft in waves. First have them correct one type of mistake, such as individual words, and then ask them to correct larger chunks of text. This may even be necessary for higher-level students at the beginning, but it is important that they try to move towards making all the corrections at the same time.

Partial redrafting on one copy

To prepare students for redrafting, it may be better to have them write or type double spaced, which then makes it easier for them and for you to see the text and insert changes. It is perhaps better to start with a short text and then move on to a longer text, or agree to focus on just part of a longer text. The corrections can be written in the margin. Then give them time to make the necessary changes above the text.

A concern is always how the text looks, but as in the case of roadworks, some mess must be expected. You could ask your students to use pencil when they write by hand and then rub out changes, but by doing this the original text will be lost. An alternative is to ask your students to write in pen and do the corrections manually in pencil. The corrections can then be rubbed out without the original text being lost and having to be called up again. If you or the students are concerned about the physical appearance of practice writing you can allow them to make a final clean copy. To show students the effect of redrafting, see Activity 7.4.

Keeping records of redrafting

As redrafting is a record of progress, try to encourage students to keep all the work you have corrected, in order. To help them do this you could insist that they number and/or date every piece of work handed in. You could also tell them that you would like to see their collection of essays periodically, say once every month. Even with a small class, wading through files is time-consuming. So tell them that you will look at their work in class. All you have to do is flick through and see that the main pieces are there.

One way to make use of students' corrected work is to ask them to use it to train themselves in self-correction. If students have typed their work and you have corrected it by tracking on the computer or you have corrected it manually, you can ask them by way of revision to look at the original text at a later date and try to correct it. They can then compare the text with the corrected version. This will help them check if they have overcome certain habitual mistakes. This also helps students build confidence in themselves and shows how much they have learnt.

Good practice 7.1

Using peer support to foster independent redrafting

Pedro, in his late teens, is from Ecuador and is of Cuban origin. He is studying English at a school in Quito. His level of English is quite advanced and he has a good knowledge of the world. He likes computers and has contact with people all over the world, using English as well as Spanish to communicate with people on the Internet.

His writing is quite original with lots of good ideas, and he is very open to suggestions when it comes to feedback. However, although he is very responsive, he does not always put into practice the changes that are necessary to improve his writing. He makes lots of spelling mistakes and encouraging him to redraft homework is very difficult. Rewriting in class, where he can work with other students, works very well for him and with social contact he can turn out fairly clean copies of his work.

In order to encourage him to do the redrafting independently, he is being encouraged to redraft only part of any homework – even if it is done just before the class starts. Pedro is not consistent, but he is beginning to pay attention to his mistakes. As the class works well together, his fellow students are coaxing him to do the homework and the redrafting. The peer support seems to work well in his case.

Good practice 7.2

Tackling overlong writing and poor organization

Wei, in her late twenties, is a Mandarin-speaking student studying at a private language school. She is hoping to go to university in Australia, the UK or the United States. She speaks very well, albeit with a slight accent, and tends to err on the side of accuracy rather than fluency. Her writing is generally accurate, but she tends to miss off the ends of words – either the last syllable or the last letter.

At a clause/sentence/paragraph level, she produces some complex sentences. However, these tend to be more of a coordinating nature, rather than more complex structures. She also tends to write more than she needs to, with some repetition of ideas and not much attempt at summarizing. She started keeping a record of her mistakes without being asked, and her teacher then encouraged other students to follow suit.

To help her with redrafting at a clause/sentence level, Wei has been given a range of tasks in order to tackle the situation from different angles. She was asked to rewrite the homework within an upper and lower word limit, and she was encouraged to put a word count at the end of her work. To deal with the lack of connection between ideas, Wei was asked to map the sentences as in Activity 7.3, and then rewrite the text inserting signposts to indicate how the ideas relate to each other.

Wei works with several of the other students in her class – all Mandarin speakers, and all at slightly different levels. As a group, they are methodical and categorize their mistakes. They keep a record of all their writing, in the correct order.

The initial result was that Wei tended to overuse signpost words, and some of her sentences became overlong. However, the presentation of ideas is clearer and Wei is now working on sentence length and removing unnecessary words. The mistakes at a word level are also decreasing, which she attributes mainly to sorting out her mistakes at the clause/sentence level.

Activity 7.1

Learning about correction and feedback

Aims:
- to help students self-edit
- to help students understand feedback and respect each other in class
- to build confidence while correcting
- to help you as a teacher empathize with students

Materials: a sample/model text containing about 15 mistakes ranging from mistakes with words to mistakes with paragraphs, depending on the level of the students

Level: All, from Intermediate/B1 upwards

Time: 45 to 60 minutes

Methodology

1 Put students into groups of mixed levels and give them the text.
2 Ask them to find the mistakes. In weaker classes, you can tell them how many mistakes and what type of mistakes there are.
3 Advise them to watch out for correcting things that are already correct.
4 Once they have found the mistakes, ask them to categorize the mistakes according to severity: major, medium, minor. Ask them to decide which ones should be focused on and why.
5 Ask the students to choose a spokesperson. Call on the spokesperson in each group to give you feedback, as though you are the student who wrote the text. Remind them to state what is good about the text first, and offer suggestions for improvements.
6 In your role as a student, offer or reject feedback: *But teacher ...*
7 Ask students to discuss the mistakes generally as a class, and to say what they learnt about feedback and correction. Focus on the good points in the text.
8 Ask students to redraft the text, adding the corrections.

Activity 7.2

Style and register

Aims:
- to help students appreciate the appropriateness of language for specific tasks
- to develop correction and redrafting techniques

Materials:
- a model/sample text (polished) of a maximum of 250 words, which relates to a specific task that students have just done. The text should contain mistakes relating to either register or style, at the word level or sentence level.
- dictionaries
- students' homework on a task relating to the sample/model text

Level: All, from Intermediate/B1 upwards (but most suitable for Advanced/C1)

Time: 45 minutes

Methodology

1 Give students the text. Ask them to work on their own and identify improvements that can be made to the text from the point of view of register or style, whichever you want to focus on.
2 Set a time limit depending on the level of the class and the difficulty of the text.
3 Ask students to redraft all or part of the text using the dictionaries and any other sources they want to use.
4 Tell them they are not to talk to each other, but they can talk to you.
5 Go around the class, helping weaker students by asking questions and offering suggestions of where to find answers.
6 Encourage them to use the questions for examining mistakes, as on page 115.
7 When they have finished or redrafted a sufficient amount, ask them to work with a partner and compare their answers.
8 Ask them to try to convince each other of their corrections, and to decide which is the better answer for each correction.
9 As a whole class, discuss the answers and ask students to look at their homework relating to a similar task. Ask the whole class questions about the appropriateness of the language they have used.
10 As a whole class, discuss the difficulties of seeing different types of mistakes, especially those related to style and register.

Activity 7.3

Dealing with chunks of text

Aims:

- to increase awareness of correction at the clause/sentence level
- to improve students' ability to correct chunks of text
- to develop self-correction skills

Materials:

- a model/sample text (polished) appropriate to the level of the class. Use a text relating to a genre you have recently taught, or one you want to revise.
- a sample text that is double-spaced, with a mixture of right and wrong connection words (*however, moreover*), and with errors in coherence.

Level: All, from Intermediate/B1 upwards (but most suitable for Advanced/C1)

Time: 45 to 60 minutes

Methodology

1. Ask students to work in groups. Give them the first text and ask them to write above each sentence or clause what kind of sentence it is, eg, *cause and effect, an example*. Set a time limit.
2. Go around the class giving help.
3. When students have finished, check the answers with the whole class.
4. Ask them to explain to you the development of the text, using the notes they have made. They can also explain to you why each clause/sentence is necessary.
5. Give the students the second text. Ask them to work individually and redraft the text, writing their own corrections above the text.
6. When they have finished, ask them to compare their answers with a partner.
7. Ask them to write out a clean copy of the text.
8. When they have finished, ask them to check for mistakes.

Activity 7.4

Redrafting: What to aim for

Aims:

- to show students the benefit of redrafting
- to show the outcome of redrafting
- to show what is possible

Materials:

- a sample of the first draft of a piece of student's writing (anonymous)
- a copy of the polished final draft. The length of the text will depend on your students, but ideally should be no longer than two double-spaced pages.
- worksheet (see page 124)

Level: All, from Intermediate/B1 upwards (but most suitable for Advanced/C1)

Time: 30 to 40 minutes

Methodology

1 Give students the polished draft to read in pairs or groups. Point out that it is a final draft with no mistakes.
2 Ask them to identify as many good points in the text as they can – ideally between five and seven. You can encourage them to comment at word level and then move up to the paragraph level.
3 Ask them to choose at least three things they like very much. Set a time limit for this stage.
4 Discuss the points indentified by the students. Allow constructive criticism if you wish. Again set a time limit.
5 Give students the original draft and ask them to compare the two texts. Ask them to identify minor and major changes, and what types of mistake were changed.
6 Ask them to suggest other possible ways of redrafting.
7 As a whole class, ask them to discuss both texts together. Ask for feedback from each pair in the class.

Worksheet: Activity 7.4

1 Look at the extract from a student text below and:

- identify at least five good points;
- choose at least three things you like very much.

The dramatic increase in the price of food that the world is facing nowadays can be addressed not only by reducing the amount of food that is thrown out but also by other measures like searching for unexploited sources of food or even the prohibition of the use of crops for the production of biofuel.

Our world has become a throw-away society because many basic products like milk or butter have a short shelf life, so that when they go off, they cannot be consumed and are directly discarded. This waste of food on a large scale is partly responsible for the increase in the price of food worldwide.

If, for example, people buy only the amount of food they need, then there will be less waste. This can only be achieved if people are educated, for which purpose the media can be used. If television programmes show how to use food efficiently, the amount of food disposed of without being used can be significantly reduced, but hygiene factors should be taken into account to avoid poisoning.

2 Look at the same extract, before it was redrafted. Compare the two texts and identify minor and major differences, and what types of mistake were changed. Then suggest other possible ways of redrafting.

The dramatic increase of the price of food that the world is nowadays facing can be addressed not only by reducing the amount of food that is thrown out but also by other measures like find out unexploited reservoirs of food or prohibition of use of crops in the production of bio fuel.

Our world has become a throwing away society. Many basic products like milk or butter have short shelf life. When they go off, they cannot be consumed and are directly thrown away. This waste of food at large scale is partly responsible of the increase of the price of the food worldwide. If for example, people buy only the amount of food they need, then there will be less waste. This can only be achieved if people are educated and media can be used. If television programmes show how to use food efficiently, the amount of food thrown without being used. It can be significantly reduced but hygienic factors should be taken into account to avoid poisoning.

8 Reading academic texts

'Reading is to the mind what exercise is to the body.'

Sir Richard Steele (1672–1729)

Assumptions about reading

We can probably take for granted that our students are able to read, but can we assume that they read efficiently and do they all read in the same way? Similarly, can we assume that they all read well in a second language? Do they read as effectively in their own language as in English, or are they even better at reading in English than in their native language? These are questions that will inform you as your students progress through a course. Apart from the language, if your students develop not just their skills, but also their language awareness, you may find that they perform better in English than in their first language.

Even though your students may have studied to degree level in their own languages, you cannot necessarily take for granted that they are efficient/effective readers of English. The only thing that you can assume is that they can read, but how proficient that reading is will vary enormously within a class depending on factors like age, professional background, reasons for reading, the amount of reading done daily, the breadth, depth and experience of reading. You may for example have a class of pre-university teenagers where one or two students do a reading comprehension at lightning speed using a panoply of reading skills that you have not taught while the rest of the class are struggling to understand the questions. At the other extreme you may have a class where all your students read well and do comprehension exercises well, yet they are not generally efficient enough readers to go beyond a certain level. Even if you group classes according to ability there will always be a range of ability within any one class.

You might ask yourself whether the teaching strategies you need to use to improve the skills of both groups are different. Essentially they are not; but detail in the methodology may vary.

Reading skills and needs-analysis

You may want to start the first reading lesson with a short needs-analysis (see Chapter 1) where you focus on what students feel that they want and what they in fact need. This kind of analysis will benefit all students – from the diffident yet talented student to the confident yet inefficient student, and all those in-between. Your students could be given an opportunity to share:

- how they think they read;
- what reading strategies they use;
- whether they read particular types of text in (a) particular way(s);
- whether they read at different speeds;

- whether the purpose for reading affects their ability;
- whether time limitations increase or decrease efficiency;
- whether exams/tests throw them;
- whether they are proficient in one particular area but cannot switch to another;
- whether they read better in English than in their own language or vice versa, with consequences for transfer.

Reading skills can be approached from several different angles, namely the nature of the text, the purpose of reading, the reading techniques involved, the length of the text and the authenticity of the text.

Purpose of reading

'I have a class of Chinese students. Several of them read very quickly and the others are far behind. How do I get the other students to catch up?'

Just as there are questions to ask before writing (see Chapter 2), there are also questions to ask before reading. Encourage your students to consider why a reading text was written and where it is from. If your students are efficient readers, the purpose of any reading exercise will necessarily dictate how your students read. Inefficient readers may be locked into one style of reading and will possibly aim to study rather than read. The broad techniques that an efficient reader requires to operate in any situation include:

- reading for gist/skimming;
- scanning;
- the ability to jump around a text with confidence;
- the ability to predict the content of a reading passage;
- identifying the main thesis;
- identifying the author's point of view and tone;
- deciding whether the text is relevant to them;
- using the vocabulary they know;
- seeing relationships between words to build a picture;
- recognizing, even superficially, the organization, various functions and development of a text;
- being able to analyse a text by questioning the content, assumptions and inferences;
- being able to understand the grammar, eg, verb sequences and modal verbs;
- juggling information;
- being able to study in depth;
- distinguishing what information is central from what is supporting or peripheral.

Just as when we drive a car we operate automatically – following the road, noticing the road signs and looking in the mirror – so when your students read they have to be able to glide efficiently from one technique to another, without really being conscious of doing so. The problem for the teacher is ascertaining which of the broad reading skills or sub-skills students have. The safest way to approach this is to assume nothing and ask students what they can or cannot do.

Building an accurate picture

As well as being able to move around a text at speed, there is also a need for students to read a text more closely, to build an accurate or detailed picture (see Activity 8.1). Using the techniques described below will help your students build as accurate a picture as a text demands for general academic reading purposes.

Reading versus studying and what not to read

Teacher: *Aren't we cheating our students by not reading everything – somehow short-changing them?*

If your students are to become efficient readers and approach reading using the techniques above, they need to learn as much about what *not* to read as about what to read. With the wealth of information available at our fingertips, none of us can afford the time to linger on every word, however much we might want to. Your students need to be able to sift through large amounts of information, locating and selecting relevant details, whilst discarding whatever is irrelevant to their purposes. Setting a time limit for the reading exercises your students do, or exposing them to information for only a short time, will help stop your students over-focusing on background information and non-essential words or details, and help them concentrate on what is important.

So that your students eventually react automatically, like the car driver, teaching and refining the skills on pages 125 and 126 and then reinforcing them over a period of time is essential. In so doing, your students' flexibility and confidence will grow. Some of these skills may seem strange to students who come from educational and/or cultural traditions where reading is equated with learning and studying, rather than extracting and manipulating information.

Examining how your students read

To bring all students up to or at least near the speed of the most efficient readers, discrete reading skills need to be taught. The most efficient students will benefit too, in that they will be more aware of what they are doing and perhaps even adapt the techniques you have taught them in class.

When you find out how your students read for gist, for example, it may be a revelation. You could tell them to read a passage for gist, without explaining how to do it, and then watch them as they read. Ask yourself the following questions:

Do they skim slowly from left to right?

Do they jump at random through the paragraph?

Do they use a pen/pencil to guide them?

Can you see which words they look at, or which words their eyes linger on?

Do they go vertically through the text?

Do they look at a paragraph as a whole?

Are they underlining? If so, what are they underlining?

Asking them to articulate how they read will show you and the students themselves how aware they are of what they are doing. You could ask them, for example, to identify their skimming style with one of the following sequences:

a Reading every word
There are many ways to develop reading speed. For example, it is possible to pick the message from the text by reading just the nouns and the verbs.

b Looking at nouns and verbs only to build a picture
There are many **ways** to **develop reading speed**. For **example**, it is possible to **pick** the **message** from the **text** by **reading** just the **nouns** and the **verbs**.

c Looking for words that organize the text
There are many **ways** to develop reading speed. **For example**, it is possible to pick the message from the text by reading just the nouns and the verbs. **So** being able to read just these words **and then** come back later if necessary requires confidence.

Once you have done this, you can start to build on your students' techniques by encouraging them to use different ways of looking for gist and give them the confidence to move away from reading every word as in *a* above. A simple way of doing this is to give your students several short texts of say 100 words, on different topics. You can perhaps give them the texts to look at one at a time, or reveal the text on an OHP or interactive whiteboard for a limited amount of time. Ask them to tell you what the texts are about. It is better to provide just the text without any questions, to encourage students to focus on the text and their reading skills.

Skimming and confidence

Skimming, like scanning, does not have to be done according to any fixed pattern. In fact, the more random you can teach your students to be, the more relaxed and confident they will be when skimming and scanning.

If you have students who approach language learning and hence reading from a bottom-up approach, focusing on reading texts at the word level, it is not going to be easy for them to change to a more top-down approach, however good they are. But if your students are eventually to operate competently in an academic setting, they need to be able to move up through the following scale:

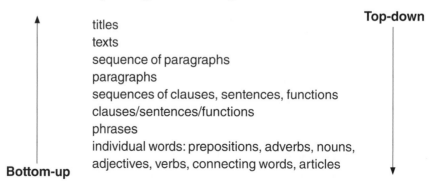

Top-down

titles
texts
sequence of paragraphs
paragraphs
sequences of clauses, sentences, functions
clauses/sentences/functions
phrases
individual words: prepositions, adverbs, nouns,
adjectives, verbs, connecting words, articles

Bottom-up

Efficient readers can move up and down the scale at will, approaching a text from different angles simultaneously. To help readers move up the scale, you can teach them to increase their reading speed. One simple pre-reading activity is to give students a fairly straightforward reading text and ask them to follow the words on the page as you read the text aloud. They will have to read at your speaking speed, which for some will be faster than their own reading speed. You can then quicken the pace. Do this for a couple of sentences, and then a paragraph. You can then read the next paragraph, leaving out the articles, prepositions and other small words. You may want to warn students in advance that you are going to leave the words out, or you could just go ahead and see the reaction. You can continue to read, gradually reducing the types of words that you read, ending with only nouns, verbs and adjectives where they are necessary to paint the picture.

Next, you can check whether the students can still understand meaning when words are left out. Ask them to work in pairs and read a part of the text to each other, saying only the nouns and the verbs. At the beginning they will be slow, but will soon pick up speed. You will find that in some cases the students will automatically pick up an adjective that is important. When they have read approximately a paragraph in total, as a whole class discuss what they have done. This activity takes a matter of minutes as a pre-reading activity. It can also be used periodically with skimming and other predicting exercises to wean students off looking only at the words one after another.

The next step is recognizing how text hangs together from a functional point of view. For further speed improvement using functions, see Activity 8.2.

Reading and marking the text

Student: *I read and then I have to read again to find the same information.*

Another way you can help your students make their reading more effective is to show them how to mark a text as they read. Everyone approaches this in their own, but not necessarily effective, way. During a reading task, go around the class and watch what the students are doing. Check:

- what kind of marks the students make on the text;
- whether they make distinctions between the words they mark, like nouns and connecting words;
- whether they over-mark the text, so that it is no longer possible to read;
- whether you can see any organization in the text from the marks, and whether the marks would help you to read the text.

To help your students realize how marking a text can help them, give them a text with questions to read. First, ask them to mark the text. Before they start to answer the questions, you can ask them to work in pairs or groups with perhaps a mixture of fast, efficient readers and those who are not so fast. You could also mark the text yourself before the lesson, and then share your version with students. What marks you use does not matter; the main thing is to keep it simple. Marks that can be used include:

- a box for important names, nouns or ideas;
- underlining for signposting words like adverbs and conjunctions;
- vertical lines at the side of the text for important passages.

An important point to mention to students is that they should not over-mark the text so that they cannot see through the marks. Highlighters are very pretty and help to draw the eye to a particular aspect of the text, but it can be difficult to draw one's eye away from highlighting.

Taking notes: Reading for writing

Indiscriminate marking or highlighting can skew note-taking. Marking a text correctly will help students make notes when extracting information from a source in order to write an essay as part of research on a larger scale (see Chapter 9). To help your students practise taking notes from a text or texts, follow the suggestions above. You could give your students an essay question, perhaps an argumentative essay or an essay within their specific field of study or discipline. Each member of the group could be given a different source text containing one or more pieces of information relevant to the essay title. Once each student has isolated the relevant information, the texts can be passed around the group for students to examine and see if they agree with the selection. Students can then put the information in order of importance by numbering the selected items.

Finding a way around a text

As your students move up through the bottom-up/top-down scale, they will hopefully see that being able to move in both directions simultaneously is important, and that it is inefficient to stick to only one reading technique.

Apart from predicting the content of a text, students can be encouraged to use a top-down approach by thinking about the type of texts they have encountered in writing (see the text types described in Chapter 4). This will help draw your students' attention to the 'map-reading' skills they can use to predict the organization of a text. If, for example, students think that everything in a text is going to be new and unknown, it will slow down their reading.

A useful pre-reading exercise is to ask your students how they think a text is going to be organized by glancing at the title or skimming the text very quickly. If you do this over a period of time using the range of texts your students are expected to read and write, they will start predicting the organization of a text automatically.

Alternatively, you could give students a list of fairly simple headings created or selected from a range of sources and ask them to decide how they think the text is organized: *Different varieties of garden shrubs; the impact of human behaviour on the urban landscape; how self-help has transformed a community in ...; the way children are influenced by television.* You can point out the limited range of text types that they are likely to encounter in academic reading and what the general features are. With more advanced students you may be able to predict the type of language used, eg classification (see Chapter 7), cause/effect verbs (see Chapter 4) and/or content words (see page 126). When students have finished the reading and any exercises, do a quick post-reading check by comparing the text with their predictions and perhaps any pointers for more accurate predicting in the future.

Some students will do this automatically and sub-consciously, but do not assume that any one language/cultural group is worse or better than another.

Question checklists for examining a text

Just as we can use questions to evaluate and analyse a writing text (see Chapter 5), so question checklists for various aspects of reading can serve as a very useful guide for your students. Encourage them to refer to the list before they read a text or as they are reading. As they become more competent, they can dispense with the list but keep it for revision purposes or as a means of reminding themselves how far they have come. You could perhaps provide students with a checklist for predicting content and organization.

Predicting checklist
1 Are there any clues about the content in the title?
2 Are there any clues/hints in sub-headings/illustrations?
3 Does the title indicate any possible text organization that I am familiar with?
4 Does a quick scan of the nouns and verbs of one or two random paragraphs trigger any schemata (a picture we paint in our heads)?
5 Have I read anything similar before?

As your students examine the inferences of a writer, they can use a critical-thinking checklist to see if the reasoning and deduction of the writer are valid. You could isolate a paragraph where a writer presents an argument. Ask students in pairs or groups to analyse the reasoning by questioning each step, and then decide whether the argument is valid and/or convincing and whether it could be changed, added to, demolished, etc. After you have done an exercise like this you can ask students to use the same process to analyse their own inferences in writing.

Using grammar

Focusing on different aspects of grammar and vocabulary can help take away the mystery of a text. You could ask students not to focus on the content or the title, or anything that would help them to predict the content, but to focus only on one aspect of grammar, such as the verbs. You could give them a text and ask them to underline or highlight in some way the main/subsidiary verbs in one or two paragraphs. They can then compare their answers in pairs and look at the tenses used and whether any modal verbs are used. The sequence of the tenses themselves also helps students see the development of ideas. It will be impossible for your students to stop themselves lifting information from the page subconsciously, especially when they are relaxed and focusing on something else.

The same can be done with connecting devices and vocabulary, focusing on organization and content respectively. See Activity 8.3.

Using what your students already know

Like you, your students bring shared knowledge of the world to the various subjects they are studying. As they write and read, they are painting a picture of the world, to which the texts they encounter belong. For example, even just lists of words, like *tree, garden, flowers, gardener,* or *plane, fly, luggage, airport, runway,* will conjure up specific pictures for your students and for you, even though they are not in full sentences. In technical terms, each picture that your students paint in their minds is called a *schema* (plural *schemata*). This *schema* is a picture that is shared with everyone that understands the words of a text that is written or read. See the text in the worksheet for Activity 8.4 on page 140, which shows what happens when we do not know what the *schema* is. You may need to remind students before and during any writing/reading task to be aware of the shared knowledge of the world as they write and read.

For reading you can also use simple techniques such as asking your students to help predict the contents of a reading text from the title of a reading passage and/or essay question. For variation, one simple technique is to create ideas by word association, eg, for an essay on reducing crime, students can be asked to create word chains of words they associate with crime: punishment, jail, cost, etc. This can be further developed by asking students to predict the types of verbs or nouns that would be expected with a problem/solution, cause/ effect organization. A further extension is to list linking devices and other features of a particular genre. So, organization and content are both being activated.

To test or guide?

If reading in the classroom is seen as merely an exercise to test comprehension, it is not surprising that it is at times difficult to persuade students to read. Reading becomes associated with testing, rather than as a source of pleasure or as a way of acquiring knowledge and information. Instead of always giving your students a reading passage with questions, you could give them an argumentative text and ask them to discuss the content. You could leave the discussion completely open without any guidelines or you could ask them to look at the passage, focusing on one or more angle(s): the content, the message, the purpose, how convincing the argument is, the vocabulary used, the assumptions of the writer, the inferences of the reader. It is important here not to focus on the grammar and to decide whether you are going to allow students to use a dictionary or not. In many classrooms, this may already be done as a matter of course one way or another after a text has been examined with questions. However, it is useful to have students discuss a text without questions, as it will appear fresher and they will not feel it has been done to death.

The activity can be varied by giving each member of the group a different piece of information or a topic to consider. Students can then ask each other about their topics, and collate the responses. Here, data, graphs, charts and visuals can be brought in.

Focusing on comprehension questions

One way of teaching students about the main focus of a text is to divide the class into groups and give them a text (the length depends on the level of your students), and ask them to make notes on a large sheet of paper about the main information in the text and the way the text is organized. For example, you could give students a text on a particular geographical feature, such as islands and how they were created. You can leave the number of notes for students to decide, or you could limit the points to, say, around seven with two or three of the pieces of information reserved for general information. Once you have done this, you can ask students to compare their notes and see how similar or different they are. Students can then be asked to create questions for the answers they have extracted. In lower-level classes, give the text and several pieces of information to each group with perhaps one piece of general information. Then ask them to create the questions.

Questions as summaries

The questions relating to any reading comprehension exercise are essentially a secondary reading task. They are also important in that they are a summary of the passage. Both of these points are worth pointing out to your students.

Bearing in mind that as we read we activate a picture of the text, by reading the questions, looking at any illustrations or reading the title or any sub-headings it is possible to construct quite a detailed picture. If you are following this procedure, it is better not to give your students the reading passage at the same time as the questions, as they will probably automatically start trying to answer the questions.

Students can be asked in groups or pairs to analyse the questions and decide whether they can predict the answers to any of them. It may not be possible to predict exact words, but it should be possible to predict the types of word and possibly a general word:

A: The Himalayas have been conquered by many expert _____.

Students should be able to predict that the answer will be a noun, probably a noun for people that is plural not singular, such as *climbers*. In this instance the correct answer is in fact *mountaineers*. Students may not know the word *mountaineers*, but the contextual clues will lead them in the right direction.

When students have had a chance to discuss the questions in groups, you can then discuss the questions as a whole class, focusing on:

- the structure of the questions;
- the type of questions (discrete/global);
- the vocabulary;
- whether the questions are related (will the answer to one contradict another answer?);
- whether the questions reflect the structure of the passage;
- whether the questions reflect the title.

Once you have discussed these points, you can give students the text and ask them to answer the questions as quickly as possible.

As a way of introducing students to this or as a means of follow-up, you may want to focus on one section of questions or even only a few of the questions.

Another useful alternative to this is to give your students the reading text, the questions and then the answers and ask them in groups to decide why the questions have been asked and why the answers are correct. The whole class follow-up can then be a roleplay where students become the teacher and you become the student(s) and ask all the awkward questions they have asked you during a reading test/exercise!

Good practice 8.1

Encouraging wider reading helps reading in the classroom

Kojo is a 17-year-old Japanese student studying at a private boarding school in a provincial town in the United Kingdom. His parents sent him to England to gain an education in English and to prepare him for entry to an English university.

Kojo is a serious student and has largely overcome the initial problems he had with studying every subject in English. He is now able to function well both inside and outside the classroom. He has always been outgoing, participating in sporting activities and pursuing a wide range of interests outside the classroom. He can read English well, but his competence is limited by a lack of practice and opportunity to read in English outside the classroom. Furthermore, there are many general topics and areas where Kojo is hindered not just by a clear lack of information, but also by the lack of a worldview. Knowledge apart, Kojo also lacks much personal initiative to read.

In the limited time available – 50-minute lessons several times a week – Kojo's teacher has faced an uphill struggle to get Kojo to read out of school hours. She has tried asking Kojo to read newspapers and simplified readers, taking him personally to the library, and encouraging him to become involved in an after-school reading group set up by several of the older students. He has joined the group and is now taking an interest in reading on his own – not just for academic purposes. He submitted reviews for several books he read as part of a library competition and won on the third attempt. His reading is improving as he can now place the reading texts he encounters in English classes in a wider cultural context.

Good practice 8.2

Learning to manipulate information

Anwar is a 30-year-old student studying computing science in Canada. He has already studied to degree level in India, and is taking extra classes to improve his English. The classes are small and the teacher is able to focus on language problems related to the individual students. After completing a rudimentary needs-analysis, the teacher finds that Anwar's level of English is very advanced and much higher than originally thought at testing and interview.

Anwar has a near photographic memory and is able to answer questions about texts in great detail. However, although he finds it easy to extract detail and can rattle off whole chunks of language, he finds it difficult to see relationships between different types of information. He can also make copious notes very quickly, with apparent efficiency. However, up until now, he has not had to deal with studying to extract, analyse, manipulate and recombine information for writing long essays.

Fortunately, the teacher does not have to teach any basic language, but she is initially daunted by the apparent scale of the task. After doing even very basic reading texts showing Anwar how the information is assembled, as in Activities 8.2 and 8.3, he is able to read more efficiently. Prior to this he did not have an understanding of the relative importance of various pieces of information in a text. It would have been easy for Anwar to be mislabelled as not being very competent and lacking in general language ability for some time, if the teacher had not probed and found his strength, ie, his memory, which initially seemed to be a weakness as it hindered flexibility.

Activity 8.1

Reading for general and then more specific information

Aims:

- to help students learn what not to read
- to help students read in depth and extract information from a text
- to contrast reading for general information and reading for detail

Materials:

- a reading text with a title and no reading comprehension questions (the length of the text variable depending on the level of the students)
- a worksheet with general headings in a column on the left-hand side of the sheet, eg, *Gist, Purpose, Source, Target, Audience, Organization, Specific details*

Level: Intermediate/B1 to Advanced/C1

Time: 45 minutes

Methodology

1 Give students the reading text.
2 Ask them first to work on their own and skim the text. Give them a time limit that will allow them only to skim.
3 Ask them not to look at the text again until you tell them.
4 Arrange them in groups and give them the worksheet with the headings.
5 Tell them to work together to make lists of information under the headings, as quickly as they can.
6 When they begin struggling to supply any more information, tell them to choose one member of each group to look at the reading text.
7 The other members ask the student looking at the text to clarify the information they have listed and add any other relevant points. Set a time limit for this stage.
8 Tell them they can now all look at the text. Then ask them to check and mark the information on the text they have correctly listed in their worksheets.
9 When they have finished, ask them to compare their marked texts with students in other groups.
10 Ask them then to choose one of the paragraphs and together in pairs or groups to make a written list of each piece of information in the paragraph.
11 Discuss as a whole class how much or how little detail you need to have to understand a reading text.

Activity 8.2

Taking a top-down approach to reading

Aims:

- to help students take a more top-down approach to reading
- to show students how recognizing chunks of text can improve their reading speed and comprehension

Materials:

- a reading text with parts of the sentences or whole sentences removed
- a list of phrases/sentences to be inserted in the text

Level: Intermediate/B1 to Advanced/C1

Time: 30 minutes

Methodology

1 Tell students to work in pairs. Give them the text with the gaps. Do not give them the phrases/sentences for insertion at this stage.
2 Ask them to decide what type of information is missing in each case, eg, a reason or an example.
3 Ask them to try to predict the content of each gap.
4 Ask them to look at the statements and decide whether they are reasons, etc. Then ask them to insert them into the gaps.
5 When they have done this, read the text together.
6 Discuss the sequence of the information in the text and decide whether it is predictable.
7 When you do a reading comprehension test in future, ask students to scan for one or two functions in the text to help them focus on larger chunks of language.

Activity 8.3

Looking at organization in a reading text

Aim:

to help students see the organization of a reading text from markers

Materials: a reading text without questions (use a text with 10–12 connecting devices)

Level: Intermediate/B1 to Advanced/C1

Time: 20 minutes

Methodology

1   Tell students to work in groups. Ask them to the look at the text. Tell them not to read the text, but to look at the organization.

2   Ask them to scan the text a paragraph at a time and look for any connecting devices like adverbs and conjunctions. When they have found them, ask them to box each one. Encourage them to use a pencil first and highlight the words/phrases afterwards.

3   Feed back with the whole class to check that they have found all the connecting devices.

4   Ask students to go through the words and phrases they have boxed and ask them to: (i) decide whether they can be left out (ii) provide synonyms and/or remove the words and change the text so that is has the same meaning.

5   Check the answers and ask them to decide what type of information the devices highlight in the text. You can do this type of exercise as an introduction to a reading comprehension/writing exercise sequence.

6   As in Activity 8.2 above, when you do a reading comprehension test in future, ask students to scan for one or two connecting words and relate them to functions in the text.

Activity 8.4

Schemata awareness in reading

Aims:
- to make students aware of the need to write within a *schema*
- to help students organize information and anchor information within a *schema*

Materials:
- worksheet (see page 140)

Level: Intermediate/B1 to Advanced/C1

Time: 45 minutes

Methodology

1 Ask students to work in pairs. Give them the model text from the first half of the worksheet on page 140, or reveal the text on an OHP/interactive whiteboard.
2 Ask students to work out what the text is about by predicting or guessing or using whatever clues they can find.
3 Give one of the students (student B) page 2, which he/she does not let his/her partner see.
4 Student A asks student B questions to clarify information in the text. Student A is only allowed to ask *yes/no* questions. If Student B works out what the paragraph is about he/she must not tell his/her partner.
5 If students appear to be taking a long time, allow student B to look at the upside-down text box at the bottom of his/her part of the page.
6 When students have worked out what the text is about, ask the class to explain what stopped them from understanding it more.
7 Then ask the same pairs to work together and add to the items 1–10 on the worksheet to the text to make it more specific, eg, *drop litter/rubbish paper/ bottles*, etc.
8 Ask students to rewrite the paragraph making the *schema* clear for a reader, or give students something else to write whilst keeping the *schema* in mind.

Worksheet: Activity 8.4

page 1

If, however, education by an advertising campaign through the media does not work, it is obvious then that the only option is to use the law to force people not to do this. Some people believe that using the law is the only way to change people's behaviour. For example, fixed penalties could be issued even when someone does something minor. The penalties could be graded according to the offence and whether someone has committed the offence before. This will help exercise people's minds, as it will hurt people's pockets and make them think. For organizations, the penalties would be higher than for individuals.

Take this city, for example. All areas could be made much more pleasant if there was zero tolerance in this matter. Furthermore, it would make the place better for people, as they would feel something about the area they live in. All it takes is to stop people …

✂--

page 2

Words in the text	Words to help explain/clarify the text
1 behaviour	careless/anti-social
2 penalties	financial penalties/fines
3 do something minor	commit a minor offence
4 organizations	shops/restaurants
5 people	pedestrians/shoppers/shopkeepers
6 areas	streets/especially parks/pedestrian areas
7 larger penalties	larger fines/closed down or banned from trading for a fixed period of time
8 this city	London/New York/Adelaide/where you are
9 better	safer/healthier
10 feel something	take pride in the area

Fold here:---

Key: In the second line: *to do this* refers to dropping litter or dumping rubbish on the streets, etc.

9 Research and referencing

Research aims and methods vary according to the type of information sought and the subject studied. The chances are that your student will be engaged in research in a field about which you know nothing, so the focus for you as an EAP teacher is on enabling him/her to cope with the linguistic demands of study. This may seem daunting at first, but actually the fact that the research student – not you – is responsible for the use of complex subject-specific terminology can make the teaching easier. Nevertheless, it will help you to understand some of the requirements of a student's research if you ask him/her to talk in general terms about his/her research, and the way(s) in which information is to be presented. This will also enable you to elicit or introduce key sub-technical research terminology.

In order to find out as much about the requirements of the research as possible, ask students to bring in the research guidelines or brief, and go through the requirements with them. Or they could download information on research procedures and requirements from their department or organization website.

An informal discussion in the EAP tutor group, or in a one-to-one tutorial, can help students articulate their particular research requirements. The questions and the table below will help students formulate ideas.

Are you familiar with these terms?

Could you explain them to a non-specialist?

Which of them are relevant to your own research requirements?

Are there any other terms you would add to this list?

What is involved in …?

What are the differences, for example, between procedure *and* approach, *or* primary *and* secondary sources?

General introductory terms	Collecting information
• *to perform or carry out research*	• *to conduct an experiment*
• *to engage in/undertake research*	• *interview/observation techniques*
• *to explore approaches*	• *data collection*
• *to formulate research questions/ design research strategies*	• *using primary and secondary sources*
• *to gain expertise in*	• *focus groups/questionnaires*
• *scope, method, procedure*	• *research strategies*
• *approach, role, model*	• *case study*
	• *single-blind and double-blind trials*
Theory and practice	**Evaluation and interpretation**
• *scientific method*	• *synthesis*
• *quantitative research*	• *standard deviation*
• *qualitative research*	• *discourse analysis*
• *establishing aims*	• *data formats*
• *theoretical framework and empirical data*	• *descriptive statistics*
• *epistemological claims*	• *hypothesis testing*
• *theoretical assumptions*	• *historical reliability*
	• *authenticity and provenance*
	• *credibility*

Types of research method

Within the broad range of research methods two major approaches stand out, and require very different language skills. The first is often referred to as scientific method and is used in science, applied science and engineering, some areas of medicine and in quantitative studies in social sciences and economics. The second is often called qualitative method, and is used in social sciences, business studies, health, education and political sciences.

Scientific method

Scientific method is concerned with the investigation of phenomena. Evidence is collected through observation, measurement and experimentation in order to formulate and test hypotheses which seek to explain the phenomena. Immediately, we can see that the language of scientific method is about precise factual information in relation to hypothetical statement. If your students are involved in this kind of research, it will help them to look at the language and organization of information in scientific journals, in the science supplements of newspapers and on websites concerned with recent developments in science such as space exploration, genetics, particle physics or economic theory. Bring these kinds of materials into the classroom and encourage students to focus on one or more of the following functions of language:

- probability, hypothesis and prediction;
- method, measurement and evidence;
- reliability and validity;
- purpose, reason and objective;
- presentation of data, statistical information;
- conclusion and result.

At the simplest level, you could ask students to underline all examples of one function and feed back to the class. This could be done as a group activity if more than one function is present. Alternatively, you could ask students to identify a range of different functions and look at the associated grammatical structures. After isolating this target language, you could also ask them to make up examples using the structures they have found to talk about their own area of study. If students are aware of historical perspective within their field, they could also be invited to summarize previous research – the work of Crick and Watson in genetics, for example.

The language of prediction and hypothesis is particularly important here, and it is a function that students often have difficulty in evaluating when reading or using when writing. See Activity 9.1.

Qualitative method

A principal aim of research using qualitative method is to examine patterns of human behaviour to determine reasons, causes, tendencies and effects. Specifically, qualitative research focuses on how and why certain decisions are made or behavioural patterns occur. Methods used to collect information include:

- detailed questioning through interviews, surveys or focus groups;
- analysis and comparison of existing documentation;
- observation of behaviour in a particular setting, situation or workplace;
- participation in a particular setting, situation or workplace.

These methods are used extensively in social sciences, education and health planning. So, what language problems might non-native speakers have when conducting qualitative research, and how can we help them? Let us look at each method in turn.

Detailed questioning

Problems include designing the right questions, understanding responses (particularly if expressed in colloquial language), collating and evaluating responses, distinguishing core information from peripheral or irrelevant detail, understanding tone and generalizing from raw data.

Analysing documentation

Problems include understanding technical terms, determining the provenance and reliability of sources, understanding the writer's purpose and tone, and quoting or citing sources appropriately in written reports or a thesis (see Chapters 3 and 8 for detailed suggestions on reading skills and analysis of text).

Observation of behaviour

Problems include understanding verbal interaction between observed participants, relating practice to theory, reporting formally on informal conversations or highly structured interactions in a formal meeting, and reporting on and evaluating observed actions.

Participation

Problems include listening and speaking skills in the setting, and reporting on and evaluating conversations or actions (often similar problems to those of observation).

As can be seen from the above, research students in these fields often need help with colloquial language. Encourage them to record interviews and interactions for language analysis in class. Also, using one of the standard upper-intermediate or advanced vocabulary books, go through typical language functions such as instructing, persuading, negotiating, complaining and apologizing.

Listening skills can be developed through intensive use of EFL/EAP materials, combined with the introduction of authentic listening texts from a range of media. Vary the tasks in much the same way as suggested for reading in Chapter 8 to include listening for gist, for specific information, tone and attitude. Students need to be able to take accurate detailed notes and interpret and evaluate what they have listened to. See Activity 9.2 for an open-ended listening questionnaire that can be used or adapted for a range of listening text types including news items, interviews, presentations, lectures and formal discussions.

EAP and research students: one-to-one teaching

Some institutions offer pre-sessional English language teaching for research students, but after that many individual students continue to need language support. Problems may occur at different stages in the research process but the basic language teaching often remains the same – a one-to-one remedial session between EAP tutor and student, either face-to-face or online.

It is tempting simply to take a research student's written work and run through it correcting all the mistakes. Although this takes little additional thought on the part of the student or preparation time on the part of the tutor, it can be time-consuming if the draft document is more than 10 pages long. Moreover, this minimal response has several other drawbacks. Firstly, if the document is merely a first draft of a section of the total research task then you can expect a lot of email attachments. Secondly, since you have demonstrated willingness to take responsibility for accuracy in English, the student sees no particular need to look at his/her own errors critically and try to improve, or at least avoid making the same mistakes again. In effect, the student learns nothing.

Also, if any of the written errors render the meaning obscure, how can you be sure, without discussion with the student, that the correction you propose actually represents what the student wants to say and demonstrates what the student needs to do in order to avoid a similar breakdown in future? Finally, there may be errors in register, organization or presentation of information, which would entail substantial rewriting on your part. You could spend a lot of time on this, yet the student scarcely benefits in terms of producing acceptable work in the future.

There are certain categories of error to look out for at this level:

Persistent grammatical errors which rarely affect intelligibility

These include the use of articles and prepositions, which often remain problematic even for advanced learners. It is useful to focus on these areas early on, and give detailed guidance, but repeated remedial teaching in this area sometimes yields little improvement.

Errors of sentence structure. The following error types can impede intelligibility:

- agreement: singulars and plurals;
- incomplete sentences, sentences without a main clause;
- sentences without a finite verb;
- failure to follow the grammar through to the end of the sentence;
- unnecessary tense change;
- word order.

For additional practice on sentence construction, taken from actual errors made by research students, see Activity 9.3. Why not collect a range of other types of error for individual or group analysis, as suggested in Chapter 7. See also Chapter 6 for errors in vocabulary choice.

Errors at paragraph or text level

Also examined in Chapter 7. There are some text organization problems which are particularly noticeable in research documents, where students have to write at length and maintain a consistent viewpoint and tone throughout. The following problems occur fairly frequently:

- repetition or paraphrasing of an argument or idea. You could take the student through the section, asking him/her to explain how the two, apparently similar, statements differ;
- juxtaposition of two pieces of information which do not apparently relate to each other, or follow logically. This can be tricky, but again you need to ask the student to explain. Sometimes a change of phrasing or vocabulary will make the connection clear; sometimes the lack of relatedness becomes apparent to the student as he/she explains. Where this is not the case, the problem may lie with the student's thinking processes in relation to the topic, so you may need to liaise with the subject tutor. See also Chapter 5 on critical thinking;
- unnecessary explanation of terminology or basic methods or procedures (apparently native speakers do this too).
- irrelevant or excessive detail (native speakers also fall into this trap). The non-native speaker may find it more difficult to gauge from the rubric or guidance just how much detail is required, and of what kind.

So, consultation is the key, and appropriate question techniques are essential. The actual question you use will depend on the subject and the nature of the student's errors, but the following provide an approach:

Could you explain this to me in other words?

So what is the difference between what you've said here and ...?

Could you give me an example here?

What do you think the writer means when he/she says that ...?

How does this example relate to your main idea?

What do you mean by the term X here? Is this a specialist term?

Could we cut this bit out? Would it make a difference?

So how does that follow from ...?

This doesn't quite work in English. Is there another way of saying that?

In English the term X is usually used when we mean ... Is that what you want to say?

Take me through this bit again. What's your main idea here?

At all times in one-to-one EAP teaching, the key is to prioritize teaching according to the potential for breakdown in communication. So, do not focus first on frequent misuse of articles if the presentation of information in parts of the text is unintelligible.

Referencing in the text: Citing sources

It is important for all students to cite sources, partly to avoid the accusation of plagiarism, but also to demonstrate understanding of work done in the field and to support and illustrate the argument put forward. For non-native speakers there may be cultural differences with regards to plagiarism, but there are also possible problems relating to the relevance or significance of the sources cited or quoted. Sometimes these appear only partly relevant to the student's thesis or may be poorly integrated into the thread of the argument. In this case you need to take the student through his/her own argument carefully, ask what the writer of the quoted material is trying to say, and how this relates to the overall argument.

Sometimes students simply need help with introductory phrases which will enable them to refer to sources in a variety of ways. These introductions may be followed by a direct quote or a paraphrase. Look at the examples in the box.

First citation

Author surname + date of publication in brackets

Smith (2002) looks at the role of Russian workers …

The following quote is taken from Crystal (2003) …

In their report/survey/article title, X &Y (date) demonstrate that …

Subsequent citations (these only require the name)

Smith also contrasts the response of … to …

In the following section on …, Crystal points out that …

Ways of introducing sources

According to X (date), …

In the opinion of X &Y (date), … (two authors)

X et al (date) examine … (three or more authors)

Similarly/In contrast,Y (date) puts forward the theory that …

X (date) states that/points out that/suggests that/contrasts/emphasizes that/proposes that/concludes that/mentions that/outlines/analyses/cites/attributes/defines/goes on to say that …

Direct quotations (these require the use of quotation marks)

When quoting a short phrase only, this may be done in the body of the text.

When Donne wrote 'No man is an island', his purpose was to …

A longer quotation is normally separated from the surrounding text, while still using quotation marks. Check with the relevant department or faculty for guidance on this but generally a quote of two or more lines would be presented separately. See the example at beginning of the section on plagiarism (page 148).

Requirements for other types of sources

Check with your department/faculty for citation requirements relating to sources with no author, articles, journals, secondary referencing, online sources, DVDs and other visual sources, personal communication, conference papers, etc.

The student may also wish to refer to a document or source of information in a broader sense. You could provide them with the following phrases:

As the graph/table/chart illustrates …

As the article/document/survey demonstrates/mentions …

The report goes on to evaluate/summarize/recommend/suggest/propose …

As can be seen from the experiment/data/diagram …

The student may also want to refer to more than one source, particularly in an introduction, or when comparing his/her findings to the work of others:

ing

earch/report/analysis is based on …

s report I have drawn on the work of …

the present study I have compared/referred to/examined a wide range of sources, ncluding …

Both X (2004) and Y (2006) have conducted experiments to determine …

Plagiarism

For a clear and concise definition of plagiarism one need look no further than Rose (2001).

'Plagiarism is the act of using someone else's ideas or words as if they were your own.'

It is not always easy to get students to understand what is meant by plagiarism. They may see the use of someone else's words as an act of collaboration or homage, a specific requirement if their tutor is published in the field, a demonstration that they are familiar with current thinking, a means to support their own ideas or simply as a tool to get them from one part of their argument to another.

There are also cultural differences in perception of what constitutes plagiarism, although this is not the only factor to consider. Uncertainty as to how to express information or ideas in appropriate English is equally important. Consequently, students rely too heavily on sources, and deliberately or unconsciously reproduce the work of others. This is particularly likely to occur where the student relies on only one or two sources. Access to information, opinion, model answers and even thesis-writing services on the Internet have considerably increased the opportunities for plagiarism, while also undermining concepts of intellectual property and copyright.

How can you tell if plagiarism has taken place? One tell-tale sign is a noticeable difference in language between the plagiarized section and the main body of the student's work. Some or all of the following may occur:

- a marked improvement in grammatical accuracy and sentence structure. Typical errors or characteristics noted elsewhere in the text are absent in the possibly plagiarized section;
- use of a wider range of vocabulary, including some sophisticated idiomatic language and/or unusual complex formal items;
- a change in style, tone or overall register;
- a slight disjunction in content between what has gone before and what comes after. The possibly plagiarized material is relevant to the overall topic, but does not quite accord with the surrounding information or ideas;
- a change of font or other formatting feature (yes, would-be plagiarists do forget this obvious giveaway).

How should the EAP tutor react to instances of plagiarism? Firstly, not all instances of over-reliance on one source, or even extended unattributed quoting, are necessarily deliberate plagiarism. Point out the need to reference the source, and ask why the student feels he/she cannot rephrase this point in his/her own words to integrate it into the argument. Encourage students to explain the information to you informally; this may help them to rephrase.

Secondly, if you feel this is deliberate plagiarism, you might point out that if you, a non-specialist, can spot this, how much more likely is it that a subject specialist will be able to do the same.

Finally, recommend that they first discuss with their subject tutor ways of integrating source material into the main body of their writing without resorting to plagiarism. Then they can come back to you for help with the language requirements.

What you should *not* do is enable the student to rewrite the surrounding sections so that the plagiarism becomes less noticeable.

Referencing: A bibliography

All sources cited in the student's written work must be referenced in the bibliography. Other sources consulted in the course of research, but not directly cited or quoted, should also be included here.

The most widely used system of referencing for publications is the Harvard system, sometimes known as the author-date referencing system. It is essential that the entries are in alphabetical order. Here is an example from Cottrell (2001) which uses the Harvard system, giving full references for a bibliography:

Miles, T.R. and Gilroy, D.E. (1995), *Dyslexia at College*, 2nd edn (London: Routledge and Kegan Paul).

Miller, A. (1991), 'Applied Psychologists as Problem-Solvers: Devising a Personal Model', *Educational Psychology in Practice*, 7, 227–36.

Miller, P.H. (1989), *Theories of Developmental Psychology*, 2nd edn (New York: Freeman).

Quality Assurance Agency for Higher Education (2000), http://www.qaa.ac.uk/ HEprogressfile; 30/5/2000.

Utley, A. (2000), 'Students Misread Tutors' Comments', *Times Higher Educational Supplement*, 8 September 2000, p.6.

Wailey, A. (1996), 'Developing the Reflective Learner', in Wolfendale, S. and Corbett, J. (eds), *Opening Doors: Learning Support in Higher Education* (London: Cassell).

The above extract has examples of different types of entries. It is useful to bring in other bibliographies and ask students to identify various examples using the guidelines below.

This is a standard order of information under the Harvard system. Aspects of presentation may vary. See notes.

Book: One author

Author's family name and initials + (year) + *title* + edition* + place of publication + publisher

Notes:

1 Title: *Usually in italics.* Some centres prefer underlined, some also want the title in bold.

2 *Not necessary with the first edition.

3 Name: Initials are usually given after the family name. Some centres allow first names.

4 Where an author has published two books or articles in one year, put *a* or *b* after the year in the order of publication. So *(2008a)* or *(2008b)*.

5 If the book is accessed online, add the website and date accessed.

6 For all dates, check whether British order or American order is preferred.

7 Punctuation and use of brackets may vary. Check with your department.

Book: Two authors

First author's family name and initials + second author's family name and initials, then as for single-author book

Note: Some centres use *and*, some use *&* between the author names

Book: Three or more authors

First author's family name and initials + *et al*, then as for single-author book

Note: Some centres ask for three authors to be referenced in the same way as two, so *et al* is used for four or more authors.

Journal article/Online journal/Newspaper article

Author's family name and initials + (year) + title of article + title of journal + volume/number of journal + page references

Notes:

1 The title of the article is not printed in the same way as the title of the journal. Usually, 'the title of the article' is in Roman script but *the journal title* is in italics. Not all centres ask for the title of the article to be enclosed in quotation marks.

2 Online journals/newspapers: The website and accessed date are added.

3 Newspaper article: The date of publication replaces the volume number.

Article/Chapter in an edited book

Author's family name and initials + (year) + title of article + in + editor's family name and initials + *ed/eds* + title of book + place + publisher + page references

Notes:

1 If the book is published in a different year from the article (ie, it is a reprint), then (year) will be given a second time after *ed/eds*.

2 The article title and book title should be differentiated.

3 Some centres ask for *ed/eds* to be put inside brackets.

4 Some centres accept a chapter number instead of page references at the end. Sometimes page references are omitted.

Encyclopedia entry

Author(s)/editor(s) if known + (year) + title of entry + in + title of encyclopedia + volume/edition + place + publisher

Notes:

1 If there is no author/editor, begin with the entry title + (year).

2 If required, page numbers will come at the end.

Corporate/official/government publications (with no named author)

Name of organization + (year) + title of document + journal title and volume + publisher

Notes:

1 There may be no journal title or volume number.

2 Some centres may ask for the place of publication.

3 For online publications give organization name + website + accessed date.

CD/Film/DVD/Video (check with your department)

Title + (year) + type of material + publication details

Also to consider, depending on the type of material:

Author or composer/producer or director/performer(s)

TV programme

Title + episode or series number + TV company + date of broadcast

Web page/Electronic image (check with your department)

Title + type of material + (year) + website + accessed date

Notes:

1 Often the year is not given in brackets here.

2 The author/director may be added if known.

Secondary reference

Author surname + (year if known) + complete reference for the source you found the information in

Other sources

Check with your department or faculty to reference the following sources:

Live performances, conference papers, unpublished dissertations or theses, dictionaries, legal and other official documents, personal communication.

Training students

To train students to use the Harvard referencing system, you can ask them to download the referencing instructions from their institution or department websites (or do this yourself), and bring them in for discussion. A more complex task could be created by taking a bibliography or part of a bibliography and cutting it up into individual entries. Students could then reassemble the entries in the correct alphabetical order. About 10 to 12 entries should be enough.

The three key points for students to remember are these:

- Use the system recommended by your subject tutor or supervisor, the department, faculty and the institution you are studying with. Look on the institution website for guidance. There are other referencing systems, so check.
- Be consistent. Check that nothing has been omitted or put in the wrong order. This also means checking alphabetical order.
- Check that the details of every citation in the text are included in the bibliography.

See Activity 9.4 for a reordering task for referencing.

Good practice 9.1

Qualitative research: The focus group

Wu Xiao Lin has recently completed a Master's degree in business administration. As part of his degree, he had to undertake qualitative research related to perceptions of advertising among a particular sector of the population. He was advised by his tutor to obtain data by using a questionnaire with a focus group, and then to present his findings in the form of a report. This research element of his course was only one of the assessed components, but it presented particular problems for Xiao Lin in terms of language.

Xiao Lin chose to research attitudes to food advertising, specifically food which is advertised as healthy. He had selected a number of relevant adverts relating to a range of well-known products. He decided to look at two groups within the higher educational establishment in which he was studying. One group consisted of students in catering and hospitality, the other group were in business studies. He hoped to get significantly different responses from his two groups, and produce a comparative report. However, he ran into problems with both groups, failing to obtain detailed feedback from either.

At first it seemed that Xiao Lin's listening comprehension and note-taking skills might be at fault, but he had recorded both sessions and had a clear understanding of the rather random information obtained. On closer examination, it was clear that his questions were the problem. They were not sufficiently precise, eliciting only general comments; nor sufficiently probing, eliciting description rather than evaluation. Also, they were not open-ended, generating brief comment and agreement rather than discussion. In order to help Xiao Lin, we needed to develop his skills in question formation. We concentrated on the following areas:

Evaluative questioning. We looked at the use of qualifying phrases, such as *To what extent ...? How far do you ...? How convincing do you ...? What are the elements in the advert most likely to persuade you to ...?* and *How effective is ...?*

Being precise. We looked at questions designed to focus on particular aspects, such as *Which particular aspect of health is the product trying to ...? Which sectors of the population do you think ...?* and *Why do you think the image portrayed is likely to appeal to ...?*

Opening up discussions. We explored phrases that invite comment, additional information or opinion, such as *Do you have any reservations about ...? Do you think your opinion is influenced by...? Can you give me any examples of ...? Have any of you personally experienced ...?* and *What makes this ad more/less successful than ...?*

We also gave Xiao Lin the chance to practise a range of his questions with a small group of EAP students, and he was able to see more clearly how to rephrase and paraphrase to obtain more informed and informative responses. By this time his original non-food-specialist group were mostly out on work placements, but another group of accountancy students volunteered, along with a second group of catering students. At the second attempt, the responses were much more detailed and evaluative.

Activity 9.1

Identifying functions of expressions

Aim: to develop skills in identification and use of expressions of prediction, hypothesis and factual reporting
Materials: Sample phrases as below
Level: Upper intermediate/B2 and above
Time: 20 to 25 minutes

Methodology

1 Put the following headings on the board, at the top of three columns: *hypothesizing, predicting, stating fact.*
2 Ask students to give examples of each – how could they express these ideas in speech and writing?
3 Ask students to look at the following phrases. They are typical of scientific discourse in a range of specialisms. Ask students what these phrases do. Do they:
   - state what experts believe/think probable but can't prove? (hypothesizing)
   - talk about future possibilities or predictions? (predicting)
   - say that this is fact, and can be tested? (reporting fact)

1 String theories suppose that ...	10 These have been suggested as risk factors.
2 A speculative solution is that ...	
3 The role of ... has already been identified.	11 These are groundbreaking findings.
4 ... may eventually play a fundamental role.	12 These factors are thought to play a major role in ...
5 These are experimentally proven ...	13 ... could help identify ...
6 Many physicists believe that ...	14 It is already known that ...
7 We may be able to determine ...	15 ... and we expect to be able to verify the results.
8 The results of the trial indicate ...	
9 ... will provide supportive evidence for ...	

4 Now ask students to think about their own fields of research and formulate statements using the phrases above. Ask them to read these out to the class. They should try to make the statements accessible to a non-specialist if possible.
5 Ask students to:
   - describe two theories that are generally accepted in their field;
   - outline two future research possibilities;
   - give two pieces of evidence or fact established by recent research.

Activity 9.2

Listening questionnaire

Aim: to develop listening and note-taking skills

Materials:

- listening resource appropriate to the level and needs of students
- guided note-taking charts with questions and prompts (see page 156)

Level: All, from Intermediate/B1 upwards, depending on the length of the text, the complexity of the topic and related vocabulary, and the speed of delivery

Time: Varies according to the type and length of listening text

Methodology

1 Open up discussion of the topic of the listening resource, and deal with difficult vocabulary to prepare students, particularly if the topic is challenging for their level. You can use visuals, elicit students' own experiences and/or expertise or use a headline from a related reading text.

2 Give out the relevant section of the chart (A, B or C), depending on the type of listening. Increase the size of the boxes to give students space to take notes. Omit any section that seems irrelevant to your text. Add any obvious supplementary questions. This is a flexible tool for note-taking development, not an unvarying template.

3 Play the CD or other listening resource. Students use the guidance questions to help them make notes as they listen. They can then confer before you obtain feedback.

Text type A: Monologue (one person speaking/reporting)

How does the speaker introduce the item?
What is the main topic? How do you know? What key words/phrases tell you?
What information/opinion does the speaker have on the main topic?
How does the speaker introduce new topics/ideas?
What are the most important points? Number them.
Does the speaker present opposing points of view?
What supporting examples/evidence does the speaker give?
Which of the following does the speaker comment on?

- advantages/disadvantages
- causes/effects
- problems/solutions
- similarities/differences
- past experience/future prediction

What is the attitude of the speaker to the issues raised? How do you know?
What conclusions are drawn (if any)?

Text type B: Interview (questioner and respondent)

How does the interviewer introduce the respondent and the topic?
What is the main topic? How do you know? What key words/phrases tell you?
What information/opinion does the speaker have on the main topic?
What questions does the interviewer ask to introduce new topics/ideas?
What are the most important points? Number them.
Does the interviewer always agree with the respondent?
What supporting examples/evidence does the respondent give?
Which of the following does the respondent comment on? Does the interviewer raise any others?

- advantages/disadvantages
- causes/effects
- problems/solutions
- similarities/differences
- past experience/future prediction

What is the attitude of the speaker to the issues raised? How do you know?
Is the attitude of the interviewer the same?
What conclusions are drawn (if any)?

Text type C: Discussion/Conversation (two or more speakers interacting)

How is the main topic established by the speakers?
What is the main topic? How do you know? What key words/phrases tell you?
What information/opinion do the speakers have on the main topic?
How do the speakers introduce new topics/ideas?
What are the most important points? Number them.
Are there conflicting views? What are they?
What examples/evidence do speakers use to support their views?
Which of the following do the speakers comment on? Who is concerned with which issues?

- advantages/disadvantages
- causes/effects
- problems/solutions
- similarities/differences
- past experience/future prediction

What are the attitudes of the speakers to the issues raised? How do you know?
Is there general agreement?
What conclusions are drawn (if any)?

Activity 9.3

Sentence-completion task: Finished or unfinished sentences

Aim: to develop awareness of sentence structure in academic contexts
Materials: handout containing finished and unfinished sentences (below)
Level: All. Intermediate/B1 students may need additional guidance.
Time: 20 minutes maximum in class. The remainder can be set for homework.

Methodology

1 Give students the handout. They can complete the task individually or in pairs. You could go through sentences 1 and 2 with the whole group as examples.
2 Tell students to analyse the rest of the sentences. Obtain feedback from pairs once the task has been completed. Accept alternative viable completions of incomplete sentences.
3 Use this as a springboard for students to examine examples from their own writing.

Look at the list of sentence beginnings below. Some of them are complete sentences, some are not. Put a full stop at the end of the complete ones. Say how you could complete the incomplete ones.

1 The Internet has changed the way we think about world news
2 The photographer who had the best photograph in the competition
3 The film medium, having declined in popularity in the 60s and 70s
4 When studying for a degree students need to plan their time carefully
5 Computer-generated visual images have gradually replaced hand-drawn ones
6 Because computer-generated images have improved in quality
7 Although digital photography has now overtaken the traditional film-based medium in popularity
8 The image of the helicopter, a tiny dot in the open sky
9 The basic technique used in order to avoid excessive distortion
10 Further professional experience is best gained at a local studio
11 This technique was developed using a commercial software programme
12 If the images can be enlarged without loss of definition

Activity 9.4

Putting references in the correct order

Aims:
- to practise putting references in alphabetical order
- to practise identifying omissions

Materials: list of references in random order (below)

Level: Intermediate/B1 to Upper intermediate/B2, no higher

Time: 10 to 15 minutes

Methodology

1 Give each student a copy of the list of references, and ask them to put the entries in the correct alphabetical order.

2 Once students have done this, ask them to identify the information omitted in four of the entries and obtain feedback.

Taylor, D. (1998), 'Changing Patterns of Tree Planting in East London Parks', in Longland, & Plummer, (eds), *Managing Urban Landscapes* (New York: File Publishing).

Tailor, J. C. (2007), 'Beech Trees in Decline', *Suffolk Naturalist* 07/3.

Taylor, F. (2003), *A Brief History of Charcoal Burning in East Anglia* (Birmingham: Townsend Press).

Tailor, J.A. (2004), *Studies in East Anglian Dendrology*, 2nd edn (Silver Press).

Tarrega, M. 'Flooding and Tree Root Dieback', accessed from http//www.klinndags.com/tar 8 July 2008.

Suffolk Wildlife Trust (2004), *A Concise Guide to Public Access Woodland in Suffolk* (Bures UK: Tye Publishing).

Tailor, J.A. & Swarbrick, R. (2001), *The Trees of Breckland* (London: Silver Press).

Tarm, Lindl 'The Vanishing Hornbeam', *The Daily News*, accessed 19 November 2007.

10 Moving from general EAP to subject-specific teaching

It is possible that you will have to teach students who make different demands on you in terms of curriculum content. Besides teaching EAP, you may find yourself teaching general English or other subjects that come under English for Specific Purposes (ESP). As the name implies, ESP relates to English for specific fields or subject areas like aviation, business, computer science, engineering, finance, journalism, medicine and music, and also includes EAP. It also encompasses English for Occupational Purposes (EOP), which is taught to people who may need English for certain aspects of their profession, although we will not cover this sector here. What distinguishes the language teaching in these fields is not just the vocabulary, as might be thought initially, but also:

- the specific skills that each field requires;
- the functions that the student has to learn;
- the organization of the written language and reading texts;
- the difference in the meanings of words in general and specific contexts;
- the frequency (high and low) of certain words (eg, *market share*, *stocks*, *capital* in finance; in music, Italian terms such as *piano*, *andante*, *mezzo*, *forte*, *crescendo*);
- the frequency of subject-specific technical versus sub-technical words or collocations, eg, *to make a profit*, *to carry out transactions*, *to play scales*;
- the special use, even misuse, of certain words;
- specific common grammatical features, eg, the passive, nominalization;
- types of language – lay and technical;
- register and style;
- the relative importance of certain grammatical features;
- the use of certain aspects of general English, eg, the need for small talk, especially when writing emails to peers, clients or colleagues;
- the need for constant updating of knowledge;
- the ability to use English in a wide range of work situations both written and spoken, in official situations, in meetings, with clients, colleagues or the public.

The students

Your students may have the ability to function competently in English within their field of study, yet interact awkwardly when required to communicate outside their specialism. Sometimes the reverse may also be the case: they can chat superficially in English, but need to learn particular language skills for their specific area of study or work. Moreover, the profile of the four main skills in EAP and ESP may be rather distorted with reading in the specific field being at an advanced level, whereas in general EAP reading is perhaps quite weak as a result of a lack of more general vocabulary and/or interest in the subject. When the skills are unbalanced like this with one or more pronounced, the student has a jagged profile. The illustrations below show sample EAP/ESP profiles for the same student. There are of course wide variations possible in the profiles of different students.

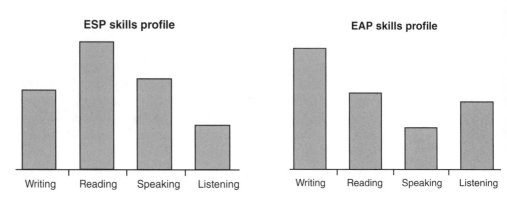

ESP students are likely to be highly motivated, especially those with a specialism in their own language. As such, they may appear more demanding and challenging than general EAP students, but you can learn to harness these attitudes to your own advantage, which will help you get over any initial trepidation or reticence.

Giving students the language tools to interact with each other

By and large, students who come to an ESP class will have done a wide range and number of activities involving interaction. But be careful about assuming that this is necessarily always the case. Any classroom activity has the potential for conflict if students do not have the meta-language required for taking turns in pairwork or groupwork, or commenting on each others' work when giving feedback.

Bearing in mind the jagged profile example for EAP above, your ESP students may have very low competence in the skills required for social interaction, and thus the skills and language required for classroom interaction. ESP students are often people working in the field, who have had to acquire a range of social skills as they deal with organizations, colleagues, clients and the public. Nevertheless, you may have to teach students the conventions of pairwork, groupwork or general classroom interaction. To do this, you can ask students to complete a simple task related to a particular field. For example, if you are teaching journalism students, ask them to work in pairs or groups and to cut the length of an article or news report. Give them a short list of useful expressions they can use to interact with each other whilst completing the task, eg, *What do you think? Do you want to add anything here? I agree, but ... But what if ...?*

Once you get to know the students better, you can arrange a problem-solving exercise. Tell students to work in groups of eight (4 x 2) or six (3 x 2), where one set of four/three students solves the problem and the other acts as monitors. Each member of the group should be monitored by another whilst they complete the exercise. They should monitor their classmates' reactions, contributions, turn-taking, listening, leadership and decisiveness. This will help prevent more assertive students from taking over, as it highlights how much they dominate a group.

Becoming specific

The list of features at the beginning of the chapter is by no means exhaustive, and you may be able to add to it from your own experience. Let us take a look at a specific field to illustrate the list. For example, someone studying journalism needs to be able to write fast and accurately, often within a very specific word limit and to very tight deadlines (sometimes instantly). He/She also needs to develop a style, have a very good command of English, have a focus on a particular field and be able to learn the editorial conventions and to research information. These are functions of the job, as well as study, which the subject tutor rather than the EAP tutor is responsible for. However, you will need to know the conventions of a specific field in order to help your students effectively. In certain cases you may find it very useful to have EOP or ESP students 'teach' you aspects of the specialist area of study.

While these aspects of the language require a focus on writing and reading, there are times when the writing and reading will be related to speaking, eg, interviewing people, socializing and interacting with a wide variety of people such as PR representatives, event organizers or travel agents. If the journalism student is further specializing in music, arts and entertainment, he/she may require knowledge of, for example, opera, as well as perhaps Italian, French and German.

Perhaps the student is asked to produce a theatre review. A prerequisite of producing such a piece of writing may be the ability to network at specific events. So for writing to take place, all the other language skills need to come into play. As a teacher, do you need an in-depth knowledge of music and theatre to help a student like this? It can certainly help – as will an interest in journalism and writing. But what is more important for you as a teacher is to be curious, flexible and open to learning about a particular field through your own research and from your students. Remember you will not need to read music, but to help a student to write about it.

Preparing to work in the field of ESP

While you may often have a choice as to what you teach, there may be instances where timetabling dictates that you suddenly have to switch to teach business English, or a one-to-one in finance or music. You may find yourself thrown in at the deep end dealing with economics, having to get your mind around graphs, data and tables which up until now you have had little or no interest in. Here is a list of various aspects and functions of teaching in ESP that you may need to think about and which you can probably add to:

- acquiring a background knowledge of the subject itself or aspects of the subject area, like writing up experiments;
- working in a team and liaising with subject specialists;

- learning new teaching skills that are appropriate to a specific subject, like giving feedback on presentations;
- using your skills in ELT/EAP to help you in ESP, and not restricting yourself. The macro teaching skills you have are still appropriate;
- constantly challenging yourself to develop your knowledge and skills;
- being more flexible and adaptable to fit in with students' timetables;
- having a knowledge of and dealing with different types of resources such as laboratory equipment, computer software and musical instruments;
- having to focus on a high degree of accuracy in student work;
- collecting and writing materials, and building and sharing resources;
- offering different types of feedback for different subject areas;
- negotiating and adapting a syllabus to fit the demands of students. This may be very narrow and relate to only one aspect of training, like writing up business reports or describing scientific experiments;
- being a trouble-shooter facilitator rather than a teacher;
- not being limited by the physical classroom;
- being student-centred but speciality-wide;
- recognizing and drawing on expertise;
- adapting teaching to the students rather than the other way around, which may result in conflict with institutions;
- allowing yourself to be carried along but simultaneously being in charge.

Where to start?

If you have not been able to do a formal needs-analysis, it is better at least to ask the students themselves what they want, especially if you are new to the field and have been thrown into teaching a specific aspect of English at short notice. You can do a needs-analysis in class – students respond better if you make it look systematic, even if it is not. See the needs-analysis questionnaire in Chapter 1, and be mindful of the fact that students may themselves not be aware of their specific needs. Sometimes you may find yourself presented with a list of needs provided by a sponsor, say, for a law student, yet the students themselves say they want something entirely different. In this situation, you may need to talk to colleagues who have worked in a particular area like English for Law, or to a subject specialist in the law faculty, for additional input.

Teaching ESP is in some respects attaching yourself to the students and following them rather than them following you, because in many, if not most, respects, they will know their field of study better than you ever can. So you need to be adaptable and use what they already know.

This may be especially true if you are teaching students with a subject specialism in a specific department, like journalism. Let us say for example that your students have had a class/lecture on the use of metaphor in journalism. How would you follow on from this? You could give your students a text relevant to their field and ask them to identify any particular metaphors used by the writer. You could ask them to explain what the metaphors mean, either verbally or in writing. Then, ask students to cover the text and give them another copy of the same text with the metaphors blanked out and numbered. The students then add the missing words back into the text, paying attention to grammar. Or, the second copy of the text could contain errors in metaphor use, which students have to identify. This task can be adapted to focus on any particular language feature. You can also give students texts on the same subject from different sources, and ask them to compare. Alternatively, you can give them another text on the same subject but treated in a more colloquial way and ask them to compare. See Activity 10.1 for more practice in this. These exercises will help you determine the breadth/depth of your students' English and how locked into a narrow field they are.

Testing students and reducing conflict

When testing students to assess which level they should be placed at, it is worth being aware that students who come in at around A2 in a general English or academic test may score much higher on a test which deals with their specialism. This may seem obvious, but it can be overlooked during testing. If this is then left undiscovered, it can lead to frustration if students are put into classes that seem to be at variance with their competence, or vanity. An explanation may suffice, but also having a test which covers more general EAP items as well as elements of ESP can save you time, energy and possibly conflict.

You can, for example, give students a test focusing initially on general language, or elements of EAP. Within the test you could have just one or two sections based on a specific context, like business, law or medicine. Or, you could have a test focusing on the specific discipline, and then end with a more general writing and reading text. Combined with an interview, this will give a good initial idea of the level of your students and will avoid reallocation of students, thus reducing conflict in the class.

Methodology: Is it specific?

When teaching EAP and ESP, is the methodology different? Yes and no. What dictates the way you teach is whether you are teaching in a university, a college, a private language school, etc. In an EAP class, you may need to be very flexible and cater for students from a wide range of subjects and disciplines, while in an ESP class you may find yourself acquiring an in-depth knowledge of a specialist subject, where you have to be careful about overstepping the mark between language specialist and subject specialist. It is advisable to point out to students periodically that you are not a subject specialist, especially the more 'expert' you become in a particular area.

In higher education courses, there may be situations that demand a different approach:

- the input may come from the students themselves by way of requiring support for an assignment;
- you may need to liaise with the subject specialist in business, journalism, medicine, etc;

- you may want to/have to double-teach with the subject specialist, so there is language and subject specialism within the classroom at the same time (there may even be more than one language and one subject specialist in the class at the same time);
- there may be greater depth to the teaching;
- the teaching may focus on teaching a very narrow, defined skill rather than the broad panoply of general skills taught in an EAP class. For example, you may be asked to focus on helping a student who is very good in other areas to write up reports;
- you may find that the students devour reading and writing materials at a much faster rate than general English students;
- you may find – especially if your students are older – that your students' knowledge of language, their subject and their language skills have become fossilized. It may be difficult to get them to develop and push themselves, as they have been comfortable until now;
- you may need to find ways of manipulating/using/developing what the students know, rather than teaching anything new;
- the activities students do may be longer and more complex (see the activities at the end of this chapter, especially Activity 10.4);
- you may need to help students develop very particular skills, like speed and accuracy in journalism.

Manipulating specialist knowledge

The types of activities that you would normally do in an EAP class are relevant in an ESP class, but there are some that are specific to each field and thus require different approaches. For example, in an English for Finance class, a student might do a roleplay that requires him/her to read and explain particular financial services to a layperson. Alternatively, the students might have to report to a specialist client, and then answer the client's questions. The first activity requires an ability to translate intra-language (change the register, style and language content) and the second requires more formal language input. The interplay between the different skills will be crucial, because if the explanation/presentation in each case is inappropriate the communication process breaks down.

There will necessarily be gradations of specific language input in each situation, with the early stages being perhaps more difficult for those students with less exposure to general English. Those wanting to enter financial services, but who have little knowledge of the field, will also be placed at a disadvantage in any classroom activity.

The methodology of language input will be similar to a general language class with pairwork/groupwork. But an activity like the one described at the beginning of this section requires more time to prepare, more time to organize, more energy to monitor, flexibility, an awareness of non-specialist and specialist knowledge, an ability to control entrenched ideas between knowledgeable students, balancing comments about language and knowledge, and making sure that the comments about the specific discipline do not distort the students' knowledge (particularly dangerous in medicine). There may need to be a lot of language preparation, theoretical reading input and homework preparation before you can attempt a scenario like the finance roleplay mentioned earlier.

You might have students who are not just studying on a specialist course, but who are also on a work placement and need to prepare for interviews and make job applications. See Activity 10.2.

Teaching ESP and working with specialist equipment

Whether you are teaching English for music, nursing, pharmacy, medicine or physiotherapy, language input will necessarily involve practical sessions with instruments or tools of the trade. Similarly, chemistry, physics and biology will all involve some practical work that can be used to support writing and reading, and vice versa.

Let us say you are teaching English for Medicine and you are teaching a nurse to explain to a mother of an asthmatic child how to use a nebulizer. The nurse needs to give the mother a leaflet to read. To prepare students, you can give them the leaflet that comes with the equipment, plus the equipment itself or a photograph or diagram of the equipment. They can then break the information down into manageable chunks in order to give a step-by-step explanation to the mother. They can take turns roleplaying and then, at the end, check what was said against the written instructions. This will give ample opportunity for the development of spoken conventions when giving explanations. Afterwards, you can develop writing skills by asking students to write their own instructions for the same or a different piece of equipment. Activities like this are golden opportunities to focus on the interplay between fluency and accuracy in writing, speaking and reading.

Given the all-enveloping nature of an activity like this, it is easy to attach discrete activities to the task at any stage, moving from reading to speaking to writing to translating, and from technical to lay language. As activities like this bring language to life, introduce them at every opportunity. You will probably find that as students are focusing on the equipment rather than the language, their language will develop more quickly. It is worth noting that you can use the same equipment to teach the same material to different levels within the same class and to different classes, thus helping to reduce preparation time.

Not being afraid to use the students as a resource

The needs-analysis will help you enormously at the beginning of an ESP course, as you may find that you are unaware of particular needs in writing and reading. You may, for example, have had a lot of practice in teaching students to write musical or literary criticisms but are now confronted with financial recovery plans or reports. How do you go about addressing this?

You may be lucky to find a coursebook or material on the web which fits your students' needs, but your best resource is more likely to be the students themselves.

When you carry out a needs-analysis, your students can tell you exactly what they want, allowing you to omit materials that are not relevant and produce lessons that are highly focused. This sometimes takes away some of the need for making decisions about the contents of a course but it does not mean that you can ignore the syllabus and course design.

ESP students may be highly motivated and stimulating to work with, but they can also be very demanding and challenging. You need to be very careful that the students do not take over and control the direction of the class, no matter how much more they know about a subject than you do. You may not be familiar with, for example, the requirements of a business or a journalism course, but you will pick up on areas that your students may not realize they need. It is therefore about creating opportunities for your students to see where they are deficient in language. A student who can read and understand a report or textbook with great ease may not understand why they cannot write well. See Activity 10.3.

Student-focused teaching for ESP

Teaching needs to be very student-centred, working closely with the student to develop the different language skills. You may find that you are not actually teaching any new language, but instead rearranging and repacking language that is already there, and adding new language as necessary. You yourself will also be learning new language in order to help your students.

Managing time and selecting materials

'Will the workload ever slacken off?'

One element that is crucial in preparing for any ESP class is time. This may or may not be recognized as crucial by the institution in which you work. You may be given a teaching slot of anything from 45 minutes to three hours and be asked to teach an individual student in a tutorial or a class in a seminar setting. You may be asked to focus on one skill – for example, speaking, for two hours; or writing, for two to three hours. But how much time do you need to devote to preparing for the class?

Let us say you are preparing for a class where students are trying to create a business plan. Even if the lesson is focused on oral communication skills, you may need a considerable amount of reading material on which to base student input. You may be lucky in that the coursebook you are using has the exact material you want, or the institution has the syllabus, scheme of work and materials already in place. However, more often than not you will find yourself trawling through various sources like books, journals, websites and newspapers, searching for sources of information to create the ever-elusive perfect set of materials. Searching out materials in this way may be extremely time-hungry, using up all of your time allocation for teaching preparation for a week. The same however may apply to using a coursebook, because you may have student input material that is very knowledge-dense – as opposed to language-dense – which will require time for you as a teacher to get your mind around.

At the beginning of any process like this, you need to be aware of how much time you have available during work hours and how much of your own time you are prepared to devote to course preparation. It is very difficult to quantify preparation, but preparation for a two-hour lesson could take an experienced teacher new to ESP anything from an hour to two or three hours. It may therefore be a good idea to keep a rough tally of the hours you spend. As time goes on you may find that as your interest grows, the amount of time spent on preparation remains the same, or you spend less time on the immediate tasks and more time on background information. It is useful to keep materials that you have collected yourself and indeed materials you have written yourself during your own time separate from those collected during the institution's time. It is in your own interests to clarify with your institution exactly who owns the materials you produce, at the beginning rather than after you have committed yourself to the process.

As you collect, develop and even write materials, keep a paper record of sources. It is so easy to use a text where website details have been removed or book sources where you forget which book it is taken from. For web pages, it is advisable to have a copy of the full page with references included, not just a PDF of the file. Otherwise, you can find yourself months down the line searching for the text all over again, especially if you have to acknowledge a work or compile a bibliography. At all times when sourcing materials, bear in mind the issue of copyright and any guidelines from the institution(s) you work in.

Managing knowledge density

Knowledge density – by this we mean the sheer volume of subject-specific information – can be off-putting for a teacher who is thrown into teaching English for a subject about which he/she has little knowledge or experience. Despite the amount of work involved, the challenge is very rewarding, especially for those of us who want to remain teachers and not become managers. Interest may in turn create a danger in that the density of the knowledge may lead you away from your focus more frequently than in more general research. It is important we all feel confident in front of our students, but remember to use the students as a resource and remind them that you are not a specialist in their subject area. Where you are coming into a department as a trouble-shooter for a particular language problem, you can rely on the subject specialist in the department for backup and support.

One aspect of using students as a resource is to rely on them to help you with clarification. Obviously, you do not want to undermine their confidence in you as a teacher, but a few discreet questions here and there to individuals, coupled with absorbing as much information as possible in class, will help you build up your own knowledge. In fact rather than undermining yourself, you are more likely to find that asking your students knowledge-based questions makes them feel valued and motivated. Acquiring a grasp of ESP will not just involve vocabulary but a range of theories, systems and specialist procedures, and it is important to gauge whether you can, time-wise and interest-wise, just dip superficially into any of these initially and build up depth as you go along. See Activity 10.4.

Finally, if you have built up a body of materials over the year, expending a lot of time and energy in the process, it seems only right that you should have some benefit by having materials ready the second time around. If you are interested in a particular specialist subject, you will benefit, as will your students, from teaching and adapting the materials one, two or more times rather than teaching in a completely new area. However, the institution you work in may make the final decision rather than the teacher.

The subject specialist

'How do I ease myself into a specialist area if I have never taught it before?'

Apart from quick immersion in the subject via textbooks, you may be lucky enough to have access to a subject specialist, who may have time to give you a few pointers, share materials with you or allow you to sit in on classes where your students are being taught. You can then 're-teach' any writing and reading material from a language point of view.

Let us say you are in a law seminar, where your students are dealing with drawing up trust deeds. The language used here is very formal and archaic, with lots of fixed phrases, collocations and Latin expressions which are rarely used outside the legal profession and which you have never seen before. You could, for example, use a sample document or a series of short texts containing some Latin phrases. Put the students into groups and ask them to underline all the Latin phrases or all the specifically legal phrases that cannot be changed because they are part of the formula(e) of the document. Students could then prepare their own verbal or written explanations of the terms with or without the use of (legal) dictionaries. You could ask each group in turn or individuals at random to choose a term and explain it, following up with general discussion or clarification. This activity allows you to learn some subject-specific knowledge, and you will therefore need to allow the students to assume a certain amount of control. However, it should be you who controls the time. You might want to use a stopwatch here, to help you in time management.

You could then ask students in the same groups to prepare an explanation of the document or extracts to a client or layperson. When they have done this, they can roleplay in pairs a consultation with a client where they translate the document verbally to the client, without reference to notes. Alternatively, you could give half the students in the class the document as well as dictionaries, and the other half just the documents. The former can prepare a translation into lay language, while the latter prepare questions for clarification of the text.

Mixed-ability classes often the norm

If your institution does not have enough students for a range of classes, it is possible that you may end up teaching a mixed-ability class with a wider range of abilities than you would normally encounter in a general English or EAP class at B1 to C2 level in the Common European Framework. This can be a problem in preparatory classes which lay the groundwork for students about to embark on a course. For those with a background in the specialist area this is less of a problem, assuming students have at least a basic competency in English at about B1 or B2 level. See Activity 10.3.

Crossing over from one discipline to another

If you have invested a considerable amount of time collecting, collating and even developing your own materials in a specialist area, you may feel reluctant to start all over again in another, new specialist area. However, many teachers do this, and the skills you have learnt in EAP and ESP will equip you to function in different disciplines.

We expect the skills that we teach our students to be transferable, and the same is true of our own teaching skills. The best advice is not to spread yourself too thinly over different fields, and to enjoy yourself.

Good practice 10.1

Teaching flexibility in ESP

David is an EAP teacher/lecturer who in recent years has been teaching EAP and business English at a university in the UK. He has a wide teaching background, ranging from teaching language and literature at secondary level to teaching EFL/ESOL in further education in the UK, Italy and the Middle East.

He successfully applied for a new job teaching English for Journalism. At first, he was at a loss as to how he could switch from teaching general EAP and business English to English for Journalism. David approached a colleague, who pointed out how he could use his EAP experience in writing and reading to talk about both skills in the context of English for Journalism. For example, he could look at how metaphors are used in particular areas of journalism, like politics, manufacturing, business or social reporting (see Activity 10.1). His colleague also explained how he could compare the use of connecting devices such as *however* or *but* between newspapers in the UK and across the English-speaking world. Similarly, he could look at how page space and target audience can dictate the coverage of a news item.

Once David realized that he had the necessary general skills, he felt that he had the confidence to adapt them to suit the particular demands of teaching English for Journalism – or indeed any other specialist area in which he might develop an interest.

Good practice 10.2

Learning to be patient

Ho Lee Mien is a very personable Mandarin-speaking student studying business English at university in New Zealand. He has a degree in business, which he studied in Chinese, and is very knowledgeable about business and business practices in different countries.

Lee Mien can speak very well and has no problem whatsoever in reading about business matters. His writing is the weakest of his skills, being only about B1 level in the Common European Framework. He is impatient in class, always giving the answers before the teacher has finished speaking. He also seems to be disruptive and asks lots of questions, not giving the other students a chance to speak.

The teacher initially thinks that Lee Mien is just a difficult student, but when she begins to become more acquainted with him, she sees the frustration behind his behaviour. He is not aware of his strengths and weaknesses and therefore does not see where he needs to channel his energies in class and in his own studies. She organizes a series of group activities which involve reading, presentation and writing (see Activities 10.1–10.4), and which teach students to interact with each other, listen to each other and speak. She asks students to identify the areas where they each have strengths and weaknesses, and where they feel they need the most improvement. She also asks students to give feedback to each other.

Subsequently, Lee Mien is much calmer in class. With the help of his teacher and fellow students, he is channelling his energies to improve his writing skills.

Activity 10.1

Comparing specialist and non-specialist language

Aim: to help students see the different types of language used in general English and in ESP

Materials: two texts: one from a formal financial magazine and one on the same subject from a daily newspaper. See the worksheet on page 174.

Level: Upper intermediate/B2 to Advanced/C1

Time: 45 minutes

Methodology

1 Give students the two texts and ask them to compare them in groups.
2 Ask them which comes from a newspaper and which from a formal financial magazine, and to give reasons for their choice.
3 Ask students to find similarities and differences in the language between the texts.
4 As a whole class, discuss the similarities/differences between the two texts, paying particular attention to vocabulary/collocations/grammatical features, etc.
5 As a follow up, give students a short text from their field and ask them to simplify it for a more general target audience.

Activity 10.2

Matching reading and writing

Aims:
- to help students write job specifications
- to help students be accurate when writing about themselves
- to help students apply knowledge

Materials:
- a job advert for a position in the students' field of study
- a specification for the job

Level: Intermediate/B1 to Advanced/C1

Time: 45 minutes or more

Methodology

1 Give each student a copy of the job specification and advert and ask them to write about their own experience and knowledge, matching it to the job specification. You may want to do this in class or ask students to do it for homework. If in class, go around offering guidance and correcting the students' work. If time is limited, you may want students to focus on just one part of the job specification, eg, relevant qualities or experience.

2 Ask students to work in pairs and compare each other's work and make any suggestions. Remind them that the description must be individual and relate to themselves.

3 Still working in pairs, students prepare questions relating to the job specification that would test that what they have written is true.

4 Ask them to interview each other, paying particular attention to the accuracy of what the candidate says bearing in mind what is written in the job specification.

5 Ask students to give each other feedback about the accuracy of what was said compared to the job specification, and the accuracy of any specialist knowledge.

6 As a whole class, discuss the exercise with particular reference to individuality, specialist knowledge and the relationship between the written information and the interview.

Activity 10.3

Helping ESP students to see their needs

Aims:

- to create awareness amongst ESP students about their specific needs
- to focus on accuracy

Materials:

- a description of a problem relating to the students' field of study (business – a failing company, medicine – a patient's illness, teaching – student discipline, finance – faulty records, etc)
- different sources of material relating to the problem, eg, graphs, photographs, written reports, data
- a list of students' names with space to write against each name

Level: Intermediate/B1 to Advanced/C1

Time: 45 minutes or more

Methodology

1 Ask students to work in groups and study the material. They should then try to solve the problem using their own experience and the information given. As they look at the material, watch how quickly they deal with it and make brief notes against each student's name.
2 Ask them to come up with a possible solution to the problem. Ask them to keep group or individual notes as they discuss. Go around the class identifying good features of the students' language and correcting any mistakes.
3 Discuss the solutions as a whole class and choose the best solution, if possible.
4 Give students feedback and ask them to identify any problematic language features themselves first.
5 Ask students to write up a brief description of the problem and the solution.
6 Correct students' written work and compare their four skills, or focus on just two, with the emphasis on showing how no one's skills are even, and how this can create frustration and hinder development.

Activity 10.4

Learning from the students

Aim: to help the students teach you about their subject area

Materials:

- a chapter from a book related to your students' field of study
- PowerPoint™ presentation equipment/smart board/OHP/large sheets of paper for display

Level: Intermediate/B1 to Advanced/C1

Time: 45 to 60 minutes

Methodology

1 Tell students to work in groups. Tell them that they are going to prepare a series of slides summarizing the information in the chapter and then they are going to present it to you and the other members of the class. Limit each group to no more than four slides. Remind them throughout of the time limit and provide dictionaries if necessary.

2 Check the spelling and language used on the slides as they prepare.

3 Once the slides are created, give a copy to each student and keep one for yourself.

4 Ask each group to present its slides and answer any questions. Make sure you allow each group the same amount of time, as far as possible.

5 Ask each student to take notes and take notes yourself.

6 Either give feedback relating only to content, or language, or presentational/organizational skills, or all three. Tell your students how much you have learnt from them and ask if you can use the material they created with other students in the future.

Worksheet: Activity 10.1

1 Read through the two extracts on finance below. Which extract is from a newspaper and which is from a formal financial magazine? Give reasons for your choice.

Extract 1

FINANCE houses set out to be monuments of stone and steel. In the widening gyre the greatest of them have splintered into matchwood. Ten short days saw the nationalization, failure or rescue of what was once the world's biggest insurer, with assets of $1 trillion, two of the world's biggest investment banks, with combined assets of another $1.5 trillion, and two giants of America's mortgage markets, with assets of $1.8 trillion. The government of the world's leading capitalist nation has been sucked deep into the maelstrom of its most capitalist industry. And it looks overwhelmed.

This industry will not be able to make money after the boom unless it is far smaller – and it will be hard to make money while it shrinks. No wonder investors are scarce. The brave few, such as sovereign-wealth funds who put money into weak banks, have lost a lot. Better to pick over their carcasses than to take on their toxic assets – just as Britain's Barclays walked away from Lehman as a going concern, only to swoop on its North American business after it failed.

Extract 2

You will understand from this that I'm probably not the man to ask whether we're all heading for the poorhouse, as so many analysts seem to believe, or whether the doom-mongers are wildly exaggerating the threat posed to our way of life by the shock waves rippling out from Wall Street and the City – waves that have already reduced some of the world's mightiest finance houses to rubble.

Detached

A year or two from now, will our streets be full of barefoot children, pushing wheelbarrows piled with banknotes to the bakery in the hope of securing the last cottage loaf – as happened in Germany's Weimar Republic in the 1930s (and happens still in today's Zimbabwe)?

Or will we all be sitting back, after a hearty lunch, dabbing vintage claret from our lips with crisp linen napkins and wondering what all the fuss was about?

I just don't know. But here is the most fundamental truth of all about modern economics: high finance has become so completely detached from anything recognizable as reality that nobody else has the faintest idea how it works either.

2 What are the main similarities and differences in language between the two texts?

Index

Further reading

Cottrell, S. (1999), *The Study Skills Handbook* (London, Palgrave).

Cox, K. & Hill, D. (2004), *EAP Now! English for Academic Purposes* (Frenchs Forest NSW: Pearson Longman).

Coxhead, A. (2000), 'The Academic Word List', *TESOL Quarterly 34* (2): 213–238.

Gimenez, J. (2007), *Writing for Nursing and Midwifery Students* (Basingstoke: Palgrave Macmillan).

Hedge, T. (2005), *Resource Books for Teachers: Writing*, 2nd edition (Oxford: Oxford University Press).

Hudson, T. (2007), *Teaching Second Language Reading* (Oxford: Oxford University Press).

Hyland, K. (2006), *English for Academic Purposes, an Advanced Resource Book* (Abingdon: Routledge).

Jordan R.R. (1999), *Academic Writing Course*, 3rd edition (Harlow: Pearson Longman).

Marsen, S. (2007), *Professional Writing, The Complete Guide for Business, Industry and IT* (Basingstoke: Palgrave Macmillan).

McCarthy, M. & O'Dell, F. (2008), *Academic Vocabulary in Use* (Cambridge: Cambridge University Press).

McCarter, S. (1995), *A Book on Writing* (Midlothian: Scotland Intelligene).

Nuttall, C. (2005), *Teaching Reading Skills in a Foreign Language* (Oxford: Macmillan).

Rose, J. (2001), *The Mature Student's Guide to Writing* (Houndmills: Palgrave).

Swales, J. M. (2004), *Research Genre: Explorations and Applications* (Cambridge: Cambridge University Press).

Swan, M. & Smith B. (2001), *Learner English*, 2nd edition (Cambridge: Cambridge University Press).

Thornbury, S. (2005), *Beyond the Sentence: Introducing Discourse Analysis* (Oxford: Macmillan).

Thornbury, S. (2006), *An A-Z of ELT* (Oxford: Macmillan).

Xue, G. & Nation I. (1984), 'A University Word List', *Language Learning and Communication* 3, (2): 215–229.